AMAZING
ANCIENT
WORLD
ATLAS

Project managed by: Tall Tree Ltd
Author: Nancy Dickmann
Consultant: Dr. John Haywood
Illustrator: Daniel Limon
Designer: Ed Simkins
Editors: Jon Richards, Nicola Hodgson
Publishing Director: Piers Pickard
Publisher: Rebecca Hunt
Editorial Director: Joe Fullman
Art Director: Andy Mansfield
Print Production: Nigel Longuet

Published in October 2024 by Lonely Planet Global Ltd
CRN: 554153

ISBN: 978 1 83758 064 4

Printed in Malaysia
10 9 8 7 6 5 4 3 2 1

STAY IN TOUCH:
lonelyplanet.com/contact

Lonely Planet Office:
IRELAND
Digital Depot, Roe Lane (off Thomas St),
Digital Hub, Dublin 8, D08 TCV4

MIX
Paper from
responsible sources
FSC™ C021741

Paper in this book is certified against the
Forest Stewardship Council™ standards.
FSC™ promotes environmentally responsible, socially beneficial and economically
viable management of the world's forests.

Lonely planet KIDS

AMAZING
ANCIENT
WORLD
ATLAS

written by Nancy Dickmann

These giant carvings of Pharaoh Ramses II at the temple of Abu Simbel in Egypt date from the 13th century BCE when the civilization was at its peak (see pages 95).

CONTENTS

INTRODUCTION

Humans have been around for many thousands of years, and those millennia have seen a huge amount of change. Civilizations have risen and fallen, but the remains and artifacts that are left behind all across the planet give us a glimpse into how ancient peoples lived their lives and insights back into the past.

The remains of the pyramids at Giza, Egypt, from around 2500 BCE (see pages 94–99)

A CHANGING WORLD

Our modern lives may seem very different from those of our distant ancestors. But visit the remains of ancient cities and settlements and you'll realize that, throughout history, humans have always had the same basic needs: food, shelter, and community. This atlas will look at how humans first learned to grow crops and rear animals around 12,000 years ago. This gave them the opportunity to settle down and form the first towns, cities, and civilizations. From these civilizations emerged new ideas and innovations, such the wheel, written language, and using fire to smelt metal and make tools, which spread quickly. We'll journey around the world to discover the people and places that shaped the world we live in today.

Statues of some 8,000 terracotta soldiers buried in the tomb of Chinese emperor Qin Shi Huang in 210 BCE (see pages 52–53)

Machu Picchu was built high in the Peruvian Andes in around 1450 CE (see pages 138–141).

This map shows the spread of *Homo sapiens* around the world. These dates are approximate and archaeologists are still making finds that change our ideas about when humans reached different parts of the world.

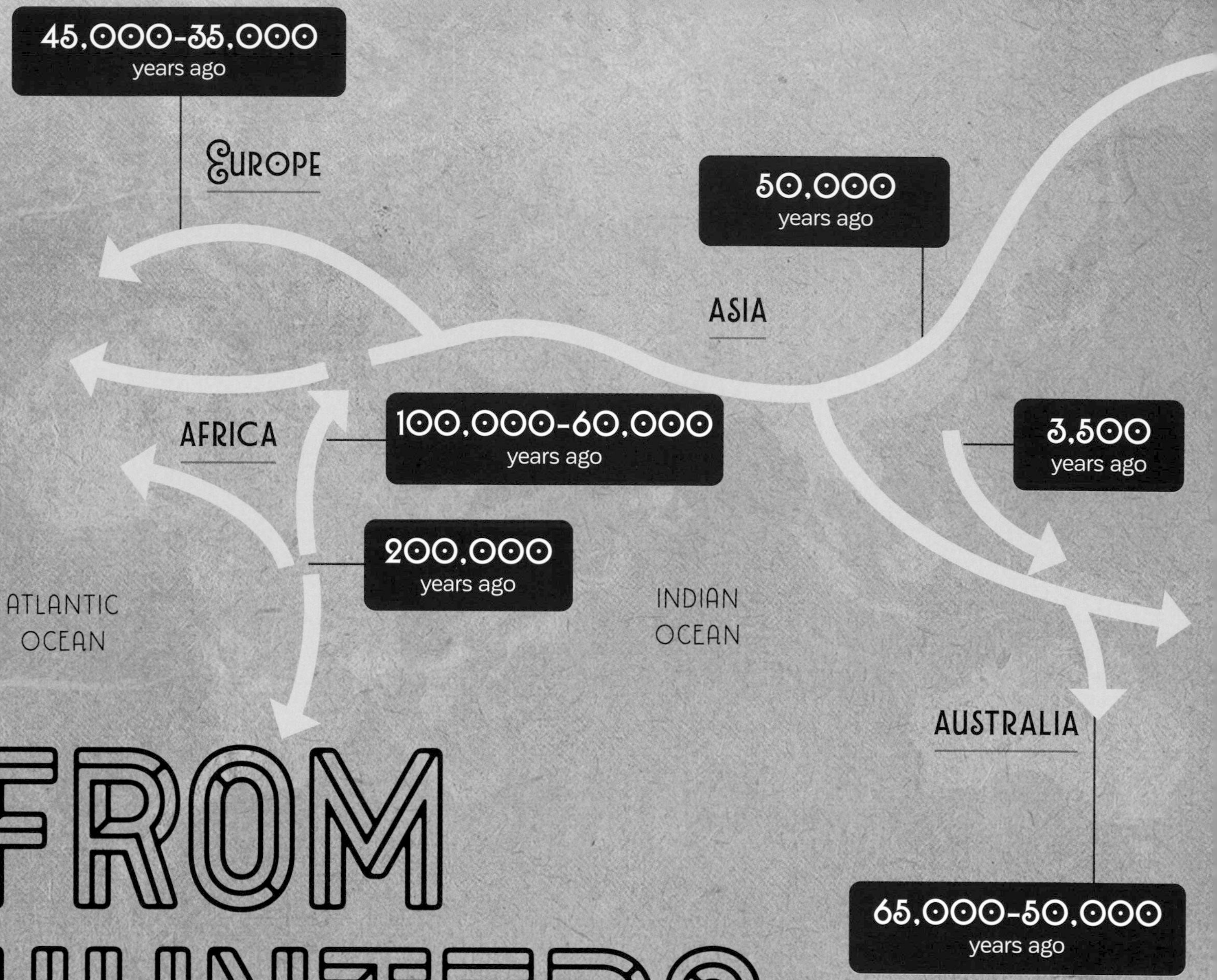

45,000–35,000 years ago

EUROPE

50,000 years ago

ASIA

100,000–60,000 years ago

AFRICA

3,500 years ago

200,000 years ago

ATLANTIC OCEAN

INDIAN OCEAN

AUSTRALIA

FROM HUNTERS TO FARMERS

65,000–50,000 years ago

About 7 million years ago, a branch on the tree of life split in two. The apelike mammals on this branch would eventually evolve into two different groups. One became the chimpanzees and bonobos that live in Africa today. And as for the other, well...that's how humans got their start!

ARCTIC OCEAN

NORTH
AMERICA

ATLANTIC
OCEAN

20,000–15,000
years ago

PACIFIC
OCEAN

SOUTH
AMERICA

2,500
years ago

15,000–12,000
years ago

OUR EVOLUTIONARY JOURNEY

One of our early ancestors was a smallish, apelike creature called *Australopithecus* (around 3.2 million years ago). A later species, *Homo habilis* (2.3–1.65 million years ago) had a bigger brain and hand bones that showed it was good at gripping things. *Homo erectus* (2 million to 110,000 years ago) came later and looked even more like modern humans, with long legs in relation to the rest of the body. *Homo erectus* may have been the first human species to use fire to cook food. The earliest human-like species all evolved in Africa. Most scientists think that *Homo erectus* was the first species to migrate out of Africa, somewhere around 2 million years ago. Our species—*Homo sapiens*—also evolved in Africa about 200,000 years ago, and migrated outward around 60,000–100,000 years ago. These early humans moved first into Western Asia, then from there to the rest of Asia and Europe. By 50,000 years ago, humans had settled throughout Southeast Asia and reached Australia, before spreading across the Pacific Ocean. At some point, they crossed into North America from Asia when an ice age made sea levels lower. From there, they spread throughout the Americas.

THE FIRST SETTLEMENTS

Early humans were often on the move. They lived a hunter-gatherer lifestyle, hunting for meat and gathering wild plants to eat. These people lived in small groups and moved to new locations to find food as the seasons changed.

PEOPLE ON THE MOVE

Relying on wild plants and animals is what made a hunter-gatherer lifestyle necessary. In most places there just weren't enough resources to support a large group for a long time. And when people had to move on to find new sources of food, they could only take what they could carry. Instead of building permanent homes, they sheltered in temporary dwellings made from plants or animal hides.

Some nomadic tribes made homes from hides and mammoth bones like this reconstruction.

A reconstruction of a
Natufian Stone Age
building in Beidha, Israel

SETTLING DOWN

Around 12,000 years ago, Earth was coming out of an ice age. The temperature was warming, sea levels were rising, and many plants were thriving. There were now some places where plants such as wild wheat and barley grew thick enough to support a population year-round, as long as the people supplemented this with hunting. This happened in the land that is now Israel and Jordan. A group called the Natufians set up permanent base camps, building houses and storage pits for the grain they collected. These were some of the world's earliest known villages.

FARMING BEGINS

The logical next step was for people to raise plants on purpose, instead of just gathering wild ones. Over time, caring for them and choosing the seeds from the best plants to save and then sow the next year would lead to bigger and better crops. Wheat (left), barley, chickpeas, lentils, and peas were some of the earliest plants to be domesticated in this way in Mesopotamia around 12,000 years ago (see page 20). At the same time, people began to tame animals. Some groups had already been keeping dogs to help with hunting and protection. Now people began to domesticate other animals to use for their meat, milk, and hides (see below).

15,000 YEARS AGO
Dogs are used for hunting (Asia and elsewhere).

10,000 YEARS AGO
Pigs are kept for meat (Middle East and possibly East Asia).

8,000 YEARS AGO
Zebu cattle are kept for meat, milk, and hides (Central and South Asia).

6,500 YEARS AGO
Llamas are kept for meat and wool (South America).

11,000 YEARS AGO
Sheep are kept for meat, milk, and wool (Middle East).

10,000 YEARS AGO
Cattle are kept for meat, milk, and hides (Middle East).

6,000 YEARS AGO
Horses are kept for meat and transport (Central Asia).

WHERE IN THE WORLD?

Scientists think that many different groups around the world developed their own farming lifestyles at different times independently of one another. It wasn't always a case of passing on knowledge from one group to another, or farming peoples moving to new locations. In the places where it happened, farming was usually the spark for cultures to start settling down and building villages, towns, and cities. This happened at different places and at different times as various civilizations learned to grow and harvest different plants, such as wheat and barley in the Middle East, rice in East Asia, and maize in the Americas.

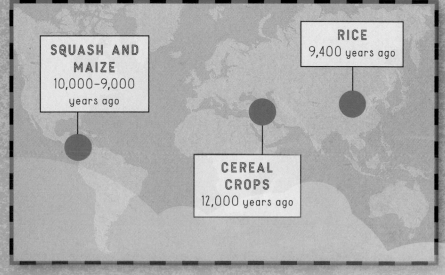

SQUASH AND MAIZE
10,000–9,000 years ago

RICE
9,400 years ago

CEREAL CROPS
12,000 years ago

WHAT MAKES A CIVILIZATION?

If you've ever been on a long camping trip, you might talk about "getting back to civilization". But what exactly is a civilization? Historians define a civilization as a group of people that farms the land, builds and inhabits cities, has a social hierarchy, and is ruled by some form of government.

How CIVILIZATIONS BEGAN

Farming was the spark that led to the rise of the first civilizations. Farmers and herders could provide enough food to support many people. This meant that large groups could live in the same place. And if the farming was successful, not everyone had to farm. Some people could become leaders, priests, craft workers, builders, or traders instead. People would buy and sell goods and services, and there would be a government to run things. These complex societies were centered in large urban cities. In fact, the word "civilization" comes from the Latin word for "city."

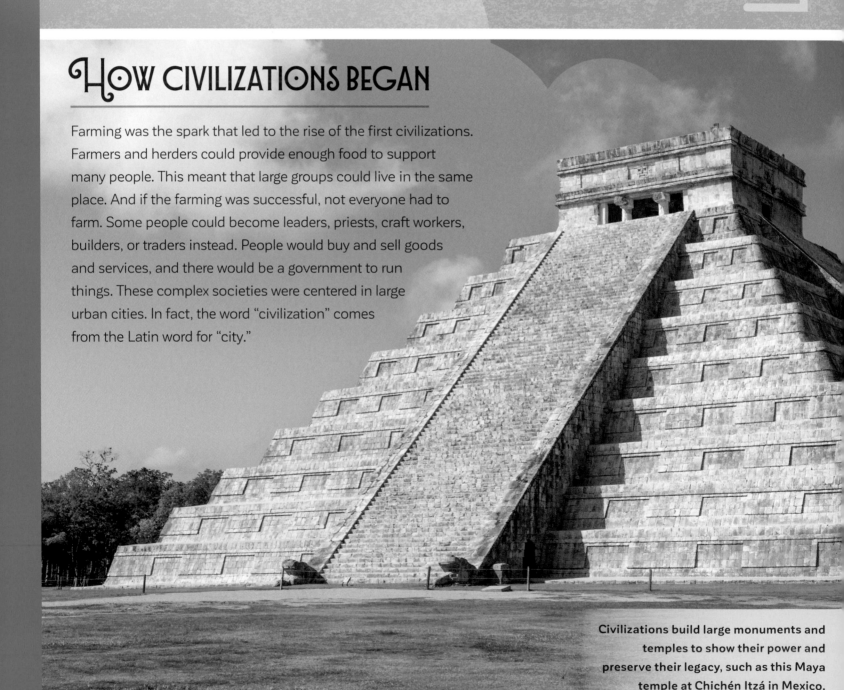

Civilizations build large monuments and temples to show their power and preserve their legacy, such as this Maya temple at Chichén Itzá in Mexico.

CIVILIZATION AND CULTURE

Culture is different from civilization. Culture refers to the shared knowledge, beliefs, and customs of a group of people. Archaeologists dig up evidence showing that people within a culture tend to make their tools the same way, or create the same style of pottery. People within a civilization usually share a culture, but not all cultures form a civilization. Archaeologists will refer to some groups as a "culture" rather than a "civilization" if they share traditions and technology, but don't have a complex organized society, a government administration, and all the rest. This book includes examples of both types of groups.

Aboriginal Australians have an ancient, complex culture, but they never had a society structured around urban centers.

HOW OLD IS ANCIENT?

If you were to compress all of Earth's history into a single 24-hour day, humans wouldn't even appear until just before midnight! We may be just a blip in the overall timescale, but in that time we've been through a lot. Historians often talk about "prehistory," which is the time before written records began. "Ancient history" comes after that, and before the medieval period. Different civilizations arose and developed at different times, so there is no fixed date that marks the boundary between periods. This book includes early civilizations and cultures from a range of time periods around the world.

People in the past used different writing systems, including Egyptian hieroglyphs like these to record their history.

TECHNOLOGY AND INNOVATION

We have come a long way from the simple stone and bone tools that our ancient ancestors used. Human history has been an extensive journey of discovery and innovation. Over the millennia, we have made huge advances, creating technologies that have changed the course of human history.

EARLY TOOLS

One of the things that sets humans apart from animals is our ability to make and use complex tools. But the materials that these tools are made from have changed over time. The earliest tools were made from common natural materials. People chipped stone to form axes, scrapers, and arrowheads, bent wood into bows, and carved bone into needles to sew clothes.

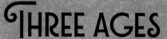

This ancient Chinese wine vessel dates from the Bronze Age, about 1000 BCE.

THREE AGES

Historians often divide early human history into three "ages," named after the material that was most important for making tools and weapons at the time—first stone, then bronze, and finally iron. Over the centuries, people learned how to use heat to release copper from its ore, and then to cast—and hammer —it into shapes. Soon they realized that adding a small amount of tin made a stronger metal called bronze. Finally, they figured out how to use iron. Iron is harder than bronze and its ores are widely available, but it is more difficult to smelt and work with.

Stone Age tools from China, crafted from bones and rocks, dating to about 8000 BCE

WHERE AND WHEN?

There is no fixed date for when the Stone Age, the Bronze Age, and the Iron Age started and ended. The change happened at different times in different places—and in some places it never happened at all. For example, in the Middle East, the Bronze Age began around 3300 BCE and the transition to the Iron Age came around 1200 BCE. In China it was a bit later—about 2000 BCE for the Bronze Age and 600 BCE for the Iron Age. This three-age system is most often used when talking about Africa, Europe, and Western Asia.

The peoples of the Americas never smelted iron, so they never had an Iron Age, though they had complex cultures, built large cities, and used other metals such as gold (right) and copper, as shown by this Inca knife (see pages 138–141).

INVENTIONS THAT CHANGED THE WORLD

Throughout history, new inventions have changed the way we live. One of the most important was the wheel, which appeared in the Middle East sometime before 3500 BCE. Calendars allowed us to measure the passing of time and the cycle of the year, irrigation systems helped to water crops and maintain a regular food supply, sails on boats allowed us to travel great distances, and concrete allowed us to construct huge and impressive buildings.

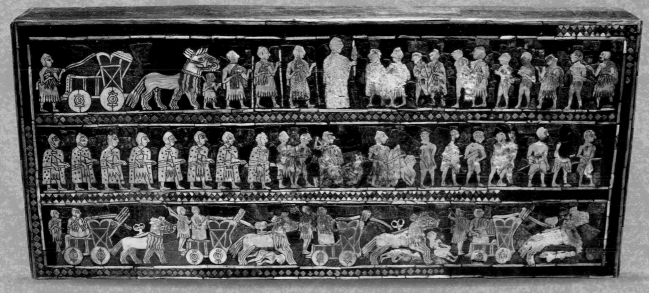

This Sumerian artifact, known as the Standard of Ur, was made around 2600 BCE and shows wheeled war chariots, some 900 years after the wheel was invented.

UNCOVERING THE PAST

It is thanks to the hard work of historians and archaeologists that we know so much about ancient cultures and civilizations. They carefully investigate historical sites to learn more about the people who once lived there.

WHAT'S LEFT?

Archaeologists use many different clues to piece together the puzzles of the past. These include the remains of walls and buildings, bones of humans and animals, and human-made objects, such as tools, jewelry, and pottery. Hard substances, such as metal, stone, and bone, are tough and more likely to survive for thousands of years. Organic materials such as wood, cloth, paper, or furs are more likely to rot away over time and be lost.

Uncovering and preserving artifacts and remains is painstaking work, much of which is carried out by hand as shown by these archaeologists scraping dirt away from a 1st–2nd century CE Roman mosaic in Spain.

TOOLS OF THE TRADE

Today's archaeologists have tools that earlier researchers could never have imagined. Remote-controlled drones with high-tech scanners can search for remains of structures through thick jungles. Satellites can also spot potential sites from orbit. Ground-penetrating radar sends pulses into the soil to find the remains of structures. Labs can analyze samples of bone and other artifacts to discover how old they are.

Aerial views of sites can reveal hidden remains buried beneath the surface, such as the remains of this Iron Age burial site in Ireland.

This midden in Argentina is formed from the remains of shellfish that were eaten thousands of years ago.

COMPLETE RUBBISH

Have you ever heard the saying, "One person's trash is another person's treasure"? For archaeologists, this is completely true. They love discovering middens—places where trash was once dumped. Middens are full of things like animal bones and shells, broken pieces of pottery, old tools, and even human waste. These objects give us clues about what people in the past ate and how they lived. By digging through the different layers, archaeologists can "see" farther back into the past.

AN INCOMPLETE PICTURE

Unfortunately, no matter how many artifacts archaeologists find, they will only ever give us part of the picture. By studying a piece of gold jewelry, we may learn facts such as how and when it was made. But it won't tell us why the person who made it chose the shape they did, or what it meant to the person who wore it. Written records tell us more about people's beliefs and ideas, but for societies that did not use a written language—or one that hasn't yet been deciphered—there is still a lot of guesswork involved.

This map identifies areas within the civilizations featured in this chapter. Turn to the listed pages to see their full extent and to find out more about them.

Ruins of Hattusa (see page 36)

ANCIENT ANATOLIA
pp36–37

Phoenician warships (see page 34)

PHOENICIA
pp34–35

ISRAEL
pp32–33

WESTERN ASIA

The earliest cities and civilizations emerged in Western Asia, in the lands that now make up Israel, Lebanon, Syria, Turkey, and Iraq. Some people call this area the "cradle of civilization," although it is only one of several places around the world where complex societies developed.

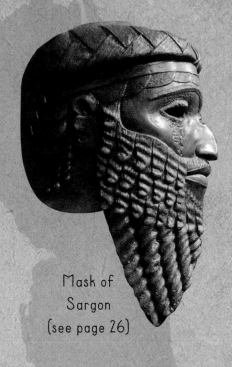

Mask of
Sargon
(see page 26)

Akkadian Empire
pp26-27

Why Here?

This area was the site of the first cities, the first writing systems, and the first use of technologies such as the wheel. But what made all these things possible was that it was also the site of the first farms, which were established in an agricultural revolution that began about 10,000 years ago. From the first small villages and towns, grand cities were soon built, and empires rose and fell. The people who lived here traded—and sometimes fought—with other groups within the area and sometimes far beyond.

Mesopotamia & Sumer
pp20-25

Zoroastrian
faravahar symbol
(see page 39)

Persia
pp38-41

Assyria
pp28-29

Ziggurat of Ur (see page 23)

Babylon
pp28-29

MESOPOTAMIA

The Tigris and Euphrates rivers flow through what is now Iraq, and they are the reason that this region is known as "Mesopotamia," which means the "land between the rivers." This fertile floodplain was the home of the world's first proper civilization, Sumer.

THE FERTILE CRESCENT

Mesopotamia forms part of a larger, arc-shaped region known as the "Fertile Crescent." It is here that farming first began, around 12,000 years ago. This region was ideal for agriculture because it had a warm climate with reliable rainfall, and it was already home to several plant and animal species, including wheat and wild goats, that were suitable for domestication. In the parts of the Fertile Crescent near the two rivers, regular flooding made the soil rich and good for growing crops.

Black Sea

Caspian Sea

Mediterranean Sea

MESOPOTAMIA

Euphrates

Tigris

SUMER

Red Sea

Fertile Crescent

Pottery from the Ubaid period is usually cream-colored, with black geometric lines drawn on it.

122885

BEFORE THE SUMERIANS

A group called the Ubaid people lived in the land known as Sumer in southern Mesopotamia around 4500 BCE. They farmed and lived in small villages where they wove cloth and made pottery. The Ubaid were the ancestors of the Sumerians who came to power around 3300 BCE. They built larger towns and cities, filled with houses made from mud bricks or bundles of reeds. They dug ditches and canals to help control flooding and to irrigate their crops.

PRIESTS AND KINGS

The Sumerians believed in several different gods, who controlled the different parts of their lives. They believed that if they offered gifts to the gods, such as a portion of their harvest, the gods would ensure a good harvest the next year. The Sumerians built temples to their gods, and they appointed priests to act as intermediaries between the people and the gods. These men were also often the rulers of cities. However, in later years, priest-rulers were replaced by kings, who were also military leaders, protecting Sumerian cities from invaders.

Another scene from the Standard of Ur (see page 15), which shows people of Ur bringing farm animals to a feast.

This statue shows Lugal-dalu, who ruled the Sumerian city of Adab around 2500 BCE.

LIFE IN ANCIENT SUMER

The majority of people in ancient Sumer were farmers. They lived in simple huts and tended their fields or flocks. Some people worked in other roles, such as scribes, priests, merchants, and craftworkers. Homes were often painted white to reflect the Sun's heat, and lit in the evening by lamps filled with sesame oil. The Sumerians used barley to make bread and beer, and their diet contained many fruits and vegetables, as well as meat from fish and farm animals.

City-States

Each city in Sumer had a wall enclosing the central area where the rulers, merchants, and craft workers lived, with villages outside where farmers lived. This arrangement, where an independent city controls the area around it, is called a city-state, and there were many of them in Sumer. Some were home to tens of thousands of people.

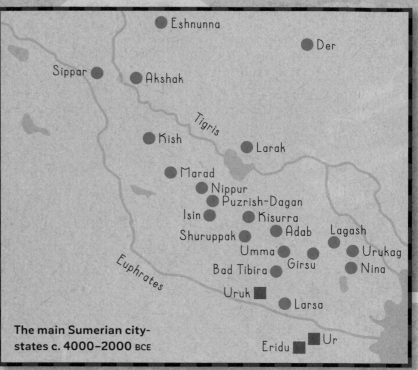

The main Sumerian city-states c. 4000–2000 BCE

This illustration of the water god Enki is based on a clay seal dating to around 2300 BCE.

Uruk

At one point, Uruk was the most important city in Mesopotamia, with an influence that extended far beyond its walls. Over the centuries, the people of Uruk built grand buildings out of stone, including a type of stepped temple called a ziggurat. Uruk was an important trading center, and archaeologists have found artifacts from Uruk at many other sites throughout Mesopotamia. There were temples honoring the queen of the gods, Inanna, and the sky god Anu.

Eridu

Eridu was founded around 5400 BCE, before the rise of the Sumerians, but they considered the settlement to be their first city. It was sacred to their creator god Enki, who was the god of water, wisdom, and creation. Eridu was built on the southern marshes of the Euphrates River, and legends tell of a great flood, similar to the one in the Bible. Archaeological digs provided evidence that Eridu probably was hit by a catastrophic flood in around 2800 BCE.

A statue of a priest-king from Uruk

GILGAMESH

The life story of one of Uruk's most famous kings, Gilgamesh, is told in *The Epic of Gilgamesh*, which dates back to sometime before 1400 BCE, making it one of the earliest written stories. It tells of a prince who leaves his kingdom after the death of his best friend and goes on a quest to find immortality. Along the way, he turns down a marriage proposal from a goddess and kills a magical bull. Historians think that there probably was a real king named Gilgamesh, who ruled sometime between 2600–2350 BCE, though it is likely that most of the stories about him were made up.

LIVED:
Sometime in the 3rd millennium BCE

A clay tablet, dating from about 1700 BCE, telling part of the Gilgamesh story written in the cuneiform language (see page 24)

UR

Ur, in modern-day Iraq, started as a small village that was founded around 3800 BCE and grew to be an important trading city in the region. At one time, it was the capital of the whole of southern Mesopotamia. Today, it is most famous for the excavations of a royal cemetery where kings were buried beside their queens, officials, and servants, along with a rich collection of items that they would need in the afterlife. Ur is also the site of the remains of huge ziggurat, which has been partially restored and rebuilt.

The front of the ziggurat of Ur was partially restored in the 1980s to show the steplike structure. The remains of the original can be seen at the top.

New Ideas

One of the reasons that the Sumerian civilization lasted as long as it did is that its people were innovators. Over the centuries, they pioneered many new technologies, such as the wheel, sails on boats, and molds for mass-producing clay bricks. They also developed the world's first writing and numerical systems, which were combined to create some of the earliest calendars.

Wheels

The Sumerians may have been the first people to use wheels. But they didn't use them for vehicles—at least, not at first. Early wheels were used for making clay pottery. Using a potter's wheel, pots and bowls could be made quickly and more easily than forming them by hand. It let the Sumerians mass-produce huge amounts of pottery. Later, wheels were used on carts for moving goods, and on two-wheeled chariots.

Writing

Clay was useful for more than just pottery and bricks. The Sumerians used sharpened reeds to form styluses to press symbols into wet clay, making them the first people to develop a system of writing. At first, these symbols were a way to keep track of business transactions. But over time, the system became more complex, allowing them to express ideas and record history. The Sumerian writing system is called cuneiform, meaning "wedge-shaped," because of the distinctive shape made by the stylus.

METALWORKING

The first peoples to use metal mainly used copper, which is often found in its natural state and is soft enough to be easily shaped. Adding tin to copper makes bronze, which is harder and tougher than pure copper. The Sumerians may have been the first to use it. They made useful items like tools and weapons from bronze, but they also used it to make statues and other works of art.

This bronze bull's head, dating from about 2500 BCE was an ornamental part of a stringed instrument called a lyre.

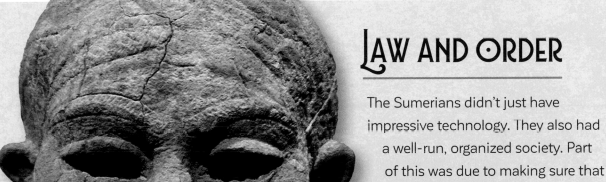

A clay jar from 4900–4300 BCE made using an early potter's wheel

Archaeologists have found thousands of clay cuneiform tablets like this one. The writing system was deciphered in the 1800s.

LAW AND ORDER

The Sumerians didn't just have impressive technology. They also had a well-run, organized society. Part of this was due to making sure that everyone knew what they were allowed to do. Ur-Nammu, who was king of the city state of Ur (see page 23) between 2047–2030 BCE, developed a code of law that was written down on clay tablets. In it, he urged his subjects to think of themselves as a single family, with him as the head. The code spelled out the punishments and fines for different crimes.

This bronze head is thought by some experts to be the Sumerian ruler Ur-Nammu.

THE AKKADIAN EMPIRE

Although the Sumerian city-states were independent (see pages 22–23), their people shared a culture and language, and at times they were united by a single king. But the next group to dominate the region would go a step further and create the world's first empire, made up of a mix of different cultures under one ruler.

SARGON OF AKKAD

Around 2334 BCE, a man named Sargon became ruler of the city of Akkad (sometimes spelled Agade). This city was somewhere northwest of Sumer, though archaeologists have never found its remains, and its exact location is still unknown. Sargon's people spoke a language called Akkadian, and they had their own culture. Sargon was known as a great military leader, and his army soon conquered the Sumerians and their king, Lugalzagesi.

This bronze mask probably shows the the face of Sargon the Great.

REIGNED FROM:	DIED:
c. 2334 BCE	2279 BCE

Akkadian Empire c. 2300 BCE

EXPANDING THE EMPIRE

Sargon—also known as Sargon the Great—had huge ambition, and he and his army moved on to take over more of the region. Some legends say that his empire extended as far as Cyprus or even Crete in Europe. This may or may not be true, but there is no doubt that Sargon united several different civilizations under Akkadian rule. He reigned for 55 years, until his death in 2279 BCE, when he was succeeded by his son Rimush. The dynasty that Sargon founded would rule for about 150 years, until the empire eventually collapsed after invasions by a people called the Gutians.

KEEPING IT IN THE FAMILY

To rule such a large area, Sargon had to delegate. He appointed trusted allies as governors and administrators in cities throughout the empire. They would ensure that his wishes were carried out. Sargon also made his daughter Enheduanna the high priestess of the goddess Inanna in the Sumerian city of Ur. Having his daughter in this important role would help build ties between Akkad and Ur through their religion.

Enheduanna wrote hymns to Inanna, some of which have survived, making her the earliest named author in world history.

A clay tablet (left) with its clay envelope (right)

INNOVATIONS

Under Akkadian rule, the region was relatively stable. Food was plentiful, and people traded goods within the region as well as beyond its borders. The Akkadians developed the world's first postal system, wrapping clay tablets in a clay envelope and marking it with the personal seal of the sender, and the name of the person it was for. The only way to open the envelope was to break it, so it would be obvious if anyone else had opened it.

ASSYRIA AND BABYLON

After the Akkadian Empire crumbled (see pages 26–27), there was an opening for another great power to take over the Mesopotamian region. Not one, but two powerful groups emerged—Assyria and Babylon. Like rival superpowers, they would trade power back and forth over the next thousand years or so.

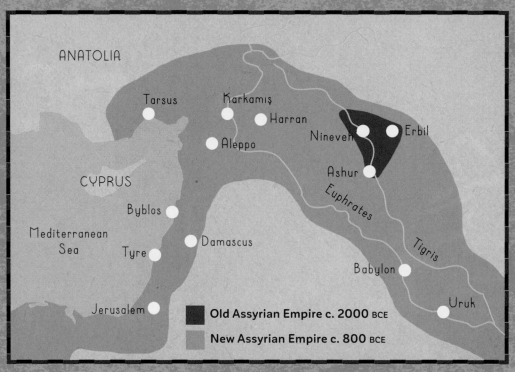

ANATOLIA

Tarsus
Karkamış
Harran
Aleppo
Nineveh
Erbil
Ashur

CYPRUS

Byblos
Mediterranean Sea
Tyre
Damascus
Euphrates
Tigris
Babylon
Jerusalem
Uruk

◼ Old Assyrian Empire c. 2000 BCE
◻ New Assyrian Empire c. 800 BCE

Extent of the old and new Assyrian empires

FROM TRADING TO EMPIRE

The Assyrian Empire started in the city of Ashur in about 2600 BCE, in northern Mesopotamia. Merchants there set up trading outposts in Anatolia, the region that is now Turkey. The Assyrians traded tin and textiles for gold, silver, and copper. This trade made Assyria rich, and it grew in power, controlling large parts of northern Mesopotamia. But after the death of King Shamshi-Adad I in about 1781 BCE, Assyria grew weaker.

ANCIENT ARMIES

Wealth from trading helped the Assyrians rise to power, but they also needed a strong army—and they had one. Assyrian soldiers were known throughout the region for their fierceness. They were also some of the first to use iron weapons, which gave them a huge advantage over opponents who were still using softer bronze. Riding into battle on wheeled chariots, firing iron-tipped arrows, and using battering rams to break down city walls made the Assyrians hard to beat.

Assyrian soldiers were protected by helmets made from bronze or iron as shown in this stone carving.

Hammurabi

As Shamshi-Adad I was nearing the end of his reign, an equally strong ruler came to power in the south. When Hammurabi became king of Babylon, he strengthened its city walls and worked on strengthening the army, too. He soon turned Babylon into a great empire, conquering Ashur and expanding his territory. Hammurabi is probably most famous for the code of laws he introduced, hoping to keep the empire peaceful and prosperous.

BORN:
c. 1810 BCE

DIED:
c. 1750 BCE

Hammurabi ruled Babylon for over forty years.

The Tabira Gate was one of the grand entrances to the Assyrian city of Ashur.

Return of the Assyrians

After Hammurabi's death in about 1750 BCE, the empire crumbled. Babylon was sacked by a group called the Hittites in 1595 BCE. Another group, the Mitanni, ruled the northern part of Mesopotamia for a time. But the Assyrians eventually made a comeback in the 1300s, pushing back their rivals. This new Assyrian Empire would last for hundreds of years, ruled by several strong kings including Tiglath Pileser I, Sargon II, Sennacherib, and Ashurbanipal.

Nineveh

Sennacherib, who ruled from 705-681 BCE, moved the capital of the Assyrian Empire from Ashur to Nineveh, on the eastern bank of the Tigris River. This city had once been a religious center, sacred to the goddess Ishtar, but Sennacherib transformed it. He had new streets and grand squares built, along with a magnificent palace. There were parks and gardens, statues, and even a zoo. The city was protected by thick walls, where people could enter through one of fifteen grand gateways.

Nineveh's gates were guarded by carvings of figures called lamassu, which had wings and a human head on the body of a bull or a lion.

The Second Babylonian Empire

After the rule of King Ashurbanipal (c. 685–631 BCE), the Assyrian Empire crumbled again. The city of Babylon had faced destruction several times over the centuries, but in 626 BCE, a new ruler, Nabopolassar, took its throne and carefully built up its empire. His son, Nebuchadnezzar II, continued this work, turning Babylon into one of the world's great cities. Unfortunately, the new empire didn't last long, and in 539 BCE it too was conquered by the region's newest power, the Persians (see pages 38–41).

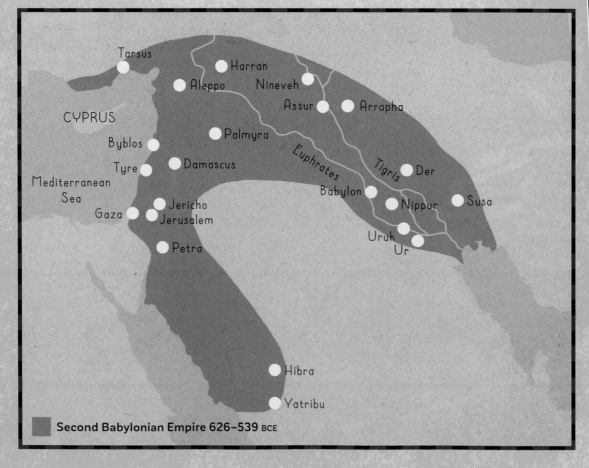

Tarsus
Harran
Aleppo
Nineveh
CYPRUS
Assur
Arrapha
Byblos
Palmyra
Tyre
Damascus
Euphrates
Tigris
Der
Mediterranean Sea
Babylon
Gaza
Jericho
Jerusalem
Nippur
Susa
Petra
Uruk
Ur
Hibra
Yatribu

■ Second Babylonian Empire 626–539 BCE

The Ishtar Gate was one of the entrances to Babylon. This reconstruction of the gate stands in a museum in Germany.

SCIENCE AND TECHNOLOGY

At its height, Babylon was known throughout the ancient world as a center of culture and learning. The Babylonians used complex mathematics to divide up land and to design military equipment. They had a counting system based on the number 60 (that's why we still divide a minute into 60 seconds) and were the first people to use fractions. Babylonian astronomers mapped the constellations and tracked the movement of planets.

NEBUCHADNEZZAR II

Nebuchadnezzar II, the son of King Nabopolassar, began his career helping to command his father's army. He quickly built a reputation as a brilliant general, winning impressive victories over the Egyptians and other enemies. As well as rebuilding the city of Babylon, his goal was to expand the empire until it had "no opponent from horizon to sky."

BORN:	DIED:
c. 630 BCE	561 BCE

A computer-generated image of how the gardens may have looked. The gardens were for pleasure, not for growing food.

HANGING GARDENS

In ancient times, Babylon was known for its beautiful gardens. They are often called the "Hanging Gardens of Babylon," and historians think that instead of actually hanging, the gardens were likely built on a series of stepped roof terraces. One legend says that Nebuchadnezzar II built them for his wife to remind her of the landscape of her native Persia. They were considered one of the Seven Wonders of the Ancient World, but archaeologists have not yet found their remains.

The Ishtar gate is decorated with images of animals, including dragons, bulls, and lions.

ISRAEL

Sumer, Akkad, Assyria, and Babylon (see pages 20–29) were all located in Mesopotamia, between the Tigris and Euphrates rivers. But there were also civilizations in other parts of the Fertile Crescent. The region on the east coast of the Mediterranean Sea is known as the Levant. Today, the country of Israel forms part of this region, and in ancient times a kingdom of the same name ruled here.

Moses with the Ten Commandments

BEGINNINGS

The Hebrew people, who established the religion of Judaism, emerged in Western Asia in the late second millennium BCE. According to the Bible, their leader Moses led them out of slavery in Egypt to settle in what is now Israel, which they called Canaan (or "the promised land"). Many historians believe this is a myth rather than a historical fact. However, other people and events mentioned in the Bible are probably real. These include Saul, the first king of Israel, who ruled from about 1080–1010 BCE.

KING SOLOMON

Saul's successor, David, brought several tribes under his rule and chose Jerusalem as his capital. When David died in about 970 BCE, his son Solomon became king. He built a great temple to house the Ark of the Covenant, which held the stone tablets inscribed with the Ten Commandments, the main principles of Judaism. He also made alliances with neighboring kingdoms.

The Bible says that David was a shepherd who gained Saul's favor by killing the huge enemy soldier Goliath.

JUDAH

After Solomon's reign, the Kingdom of Israel split in two. The northern part was still called Israel, but the southern part was known as Judah. Jerusalem became the capital of Judah, while the Kingdom of Israel set up a new capital at Samaria. The two kingdoms would sometimes work together and sometimes fight. They were never as strong separately as they had been together under the reigns of David and Solomon.

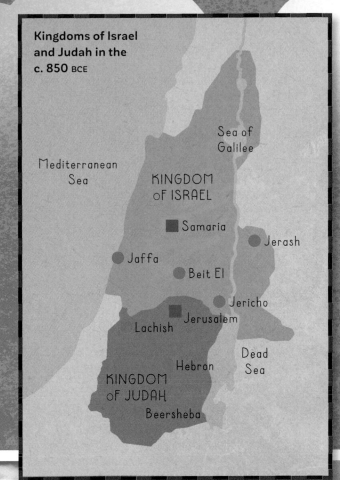

Kingdoms of Israel and Judah in the c. 850 BCE

Mediterranean Sea

Sea of Galilee

KINGDOM OF ISRAEL

Samaria

Jaffa

Jerash

Beit El

Jericho

Jerusalem

Lachish

Dead Sea

Hebron

KINGDOM OF JUDAH

Beersheba

THE END

The Babylonian king Nebuchadnezzar II (see page 31) conquered the region in around 598 BCE. His armies sacked Jerusalem and destroyed the temple, capturing many people and taking them back to Babylon to work as slaves. The people of Israel—known as Hebrews, Jews, or Israelites—didn't return to their homeland until the Persians overthrew the Babylonians and freed them in 539 BCE. But their freedom didn't last and they were eventually conquered by the Roman Empire in the first century BCE.

The Israelites rebuilt the Temple in Jerusalem, but it was destroyed by the Romans in 70 CE. All that remains now is part of one wall.

THE PHOENICIANS

As well as Israel and Judah (see pages 32–33) another civilization grew up on the Levant, in the land often known as Canaan, in the second millennium BCE. The Phoenicians lived in independent city-states such as Sidon and Tyre. But they took to the sea in a way that no other culture in the region yet had, becoming masters of the Mediterranean.

MEDITERRANEAN CITY-STATES

The Phoenician homeland was a narrow, rocky strip of land on the coast. The people found it easier to travel from one settlement to another by sea, rather than over land. Some of their cities were actually built on small islands near the coast, making them harder to invade. All this meant that when the Phoenicians wanted to expand their civilization, starting around 1500 BCE, the obvious direction was to go west into the Mediterranean, rather than east into land that was already occupied.

The cedar trees that grew in Phoenicia had tall, thick trunks—perfect for boat building.

Convoys of cargo ships were often accompanied by warships like this for protection.

SUPER SAILORS

Phoenicians were known throughout the ancient Middle East as skilled sailors. In fact, they may have been some of the first people to sail so far out to sea that they could no longer see land. A typical Phoenician ship was powered by a square sail and two banks of rowers. Some would have a horse's head at the front in honor of Yamm, the Phoenician god of the sea. There were sleek warships with battering rams on the bow, but there were also larger trading vessels. In these ships, Phoenician sailors traveled as far as Spain and perhaps even to Britain.

The map shows labels: EUROPE, Black Sea, SPAIN, SARDINIA, Rome, GREECE, ANATOLIA, PHOENICIA, Malaca, Balearic Islands, Palermo, Aradus, Gadir, SICILY, CYPRUS, Tingis, Hippo Regius, Carthage, Citium, Sidon, Lixus, Tyre, Mediterranean Sea, Oea, AFRICA, Leptis Magna, Alexandria

Extent of Phoenician influence

TRADING EMPIRE

Thanks to their ships and a reputation as makers of luxury goods, the Phoenicians set up a trading empire across the Mediterranean. They produced beautiful glassware as well as textiles, cedar wood, and an extremely expensive dye called Tyrian purple, made by boiling sea snails. They traded these goods for metals, farm animals, spices, and precious stones. Their trading empire lasted until they were conquered by the Greek leader Alexander the Great in 332 BCE (see pages 78–79).

This map shows the farthest extent of Phoenician influence in the first millennium BCE. The Phoenicians set up colonies around the Mediterranean, such as Carthage and Leptis Magna in northern Africa.

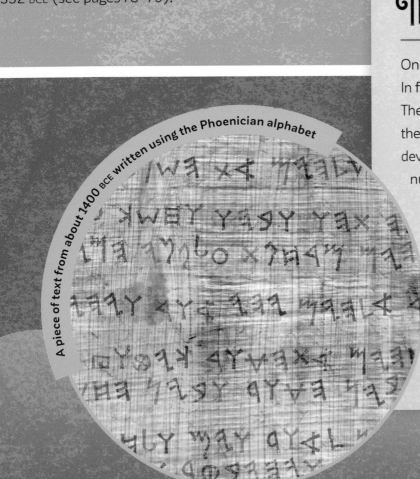

A piece of text from about 1400 BCE written using the Phoenician alphabet

THE ALPHABET

One Phoenician innovation is still with us today. In fact, it's the reason you can read this book! The Phoenician language was once written using the Sumerian cuneiform system. But they later developed a new system of letters. Using a small number of symbols that represent sounds—rather than a lot of different pictures that represent words—makes an alphabet easier to learn. The Phoenician alphabet spread quickly among their trading partners. The Greeks adapted it to write their own language, and then the Roman alphabet that we use today was based on that.

ANCIENT ANATOLIA

Located in what is now Turkey, the region of Anatolia saw the rise of several civilizations during the Bronze and Iron Ages. These included the Hittites, the Phrygians, and the Lydians. Eventually, the entire region was conquered and ruled by the mighty Persian Empire (see pages 38–41).

HITTITES

The Hittites are often mentioned in the Bible as the enemies of the Israelites. These people were based in central Anatolia. In around 1700 BCE, the Hittite king Anitta of Kussara did what Sargon the Great (see page 26) had tried and failed to do, and conquered the Hatti people and their city of Hattusa. Hattusa was then made the capital of the growing Hittite Empire.

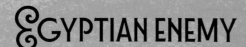
These lions stand guard on either side of a gateway to the ruins of Hattusa.

EGYPTIAN ENEMY

The Hittite Empire reached its peak under King Suppiluliumas, who came to power in about 1380 BCE. In 1275 BCE near the city of Kadesh in the Levant, the Hittites fought a great battle against the Egyptians and their pharaoh, Ramses II (see pages 94–95). The Hittite Empire came to an end not long after that, and was taken over by the Phrygians.

This carving made around 1280 BCE shows Egyptian soldiers under the command of Ramses II at the Battle of Kadesh.

Phrygians

The Phrygians took over western Anatolia after the Hittite Empire collapsed. According to Greek historians, they originally came from the Balkans in southeast Europe, but settled in Anatolia—possibly attracted by the region's fertile plains. The legendary King Midas, who was cursed with the ability to turn anything he touched into gold, was said to be king of Phrygia. Phrygia was known for its metalwork and pottery, and the Phrygians traded with people as far away as Greece and Persia. They set up a system of roads to make trading easier. The Phrygians lasted until 696 BCE, when their capital city, Gordium, was sacked by a nomadic group from the east called the Cimmerians.

A "Phrygian cap" is a style of soft hat famously worn by the Phrygians and other groups in the region.

Lydians

By around 625 BCE, the Lydians had taken over Phrygia from the Cimmerians. These people had been living near the west coast of Anatolia for hundreds of years. They traded gold, silver, fine cloth, and leather across the Mediterranean. Lydia was one of the first kingdoms to make metal coins, around 600 BCE. They were small lumps of silver or gold stamped with a design of a lion and an ox. Lydia reached its height under King Croesus, who came to power in 560 BCE. He was known to the Greeks for his legendary wealth, and was the source of the phrase "as rich as Croesus." But Croesus was defeated and overthrown in 546 BCE by the Persians led by Cyrus.

Gold coins minted during the reign of Croesus

An image of Croesus from around 500 BCE

PERSIA

Persia is an ancient name for the region that we now know as Iran. When the Persians arrived in Iran around 1000 BCE, they were just a collection of nomadic tribes, but they eventually organized and rose to become one of history's greatest empires.

This cylinder is a piece of ancient propaganda and it tells people what an able king Cyrus is, listing his good deeds.

CYRUS THE GREAT

In 553 BCE, a local Persian king, Cyrus, led a revolt against the region's then dominant power, the Medes. After his victory, Cyrus started to build a larger empire, known as the Achaemenid (or First Persian) Empire. He conquered Lydia after defeating Croesus in battle, then invaded the Babylonian Empire (see pages 28–31). As he built up more and more territory, Cyrus gained a reputation as a fair ruler. He allowed conquered peoples to keep their own religion and customs, as long as they paid their taxes.

MILITARY POWER

Under Cyrus and his successors, the Persian army was a force to be reckoned with. As the empire grew, more soldiers were drafted in from the new provinces. There was an infantry that included foot soldiers, archers, and fighters who used slingshots. The Persians also had a strong cavalry—some riding horses and others on camels. Their soldiers were well trained and the generals made good use of tactics to win battles.

Persian soldiers (shown on the left of this plate made around 450 BCE) were very successful, but they never conquered Greece (see pages 72–77).

A NEW RELIGION

In the ancient world, it was very common for people to worship many gods. Each one would control a different aspect of daily life, such as war, fire, love, or the Sun. But under Cyrus the Great, the Persian Empire adopted the Zoroastrian religion, which worshipped a single god named Ahura Mazda. Zoroastrians were expected to choose between good and evil and show their goodness through their thoughts, words, and deeds.

The symbol of Zoroastrianism, called the faravahar, shows a bearded man with one hand reaching out, with a pair of outstretched wings.

ART AND ARCHITECTURE

When Darius I—later known as Darius the Great—came to power in 522 BCE, he had a new capital built at Persepolis. Its grand buildings were made of stone rather than mud brick. Many were decorated with elaborate carved scenes and had tall columns with bulls or other animals at the top. The Persians were also known for their beautiful jewelry, made of gold and precious stones. And gold wasn't just for jewelry—Greek historians wrote about the buildings of Persepolis being covered in huge amounts of gold.

The ruins of the Persian capital city, Persepolis.

The World's First Superpower

After the death of Cyrus the Great in 530 BCE, other rulers continued to expand the Achaemenid Empire. At its height, it included Mesopotamia, the Nile Valley of Egypt, and the Indus Valley far to the east. The empire was the world's first superpower, uniting a huge range of different cultures and civilizations under a single ruler. A dynasty of strong leaders, including Darius and Darius's son Xerxes, helped keep control.

Staying Connected

Ruling over a large area is never easy, especially without today's high-speed transportation and communications. The Persians managed it by setting up a system of provinces, each one run by a governor who reported to the emperor. They used the income from taxes to build a network of roads and canals. This included the Royal Road, which stretched more than 1,500 miles (2,400 km) from Susa in modern Iran to Sardis in modern Turkey. Couriers on horseback could travel this road in nine days when carrying important messages.

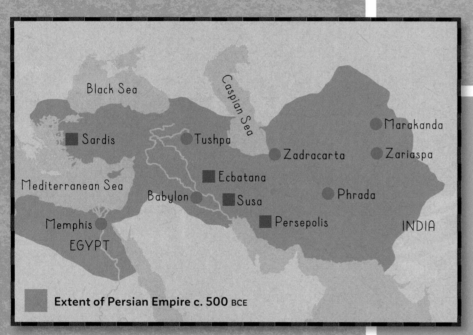

Black Sea

Caspian Sea

Sardis

Tushpa

Marakanda

Zadracarta

Zariaspa

Ecbatana

Mediterranean Sea

Babylon

Susa

Phrada

Memphis

Persepolis

EGYPT

INDIA

■ Extent of Persian Empire c. 500 BCE

Historians estimate that at one point, about 44 percent of the world's population was ruled by the Persian Empire.

A standard Persian weight dating from about 500 BCE

Persian Trade

The roads were also used by traders, carrying goods to all corners of the empire. The government helped merchants by standardizing the currency, which was called the daric. Although provinces could use their own coins and money systems, they were fixed to the value of the daric. The Persians also set up a system of standard weights and measures, to ensure that buyers and sellers got a fair deal. It also helped that the Aramaic language was used throughout the empire.

Darius the Great

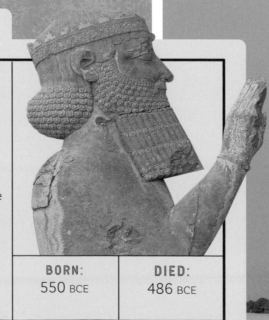

Darius was a distant relative of Cyrus and served under Cyrus's son and successor, Cambyses. He came to power in 522 BCE when still a young man and reigned for 36 years until his death in 486 BCE. Darius was an excellent military leader, and the empire reached its peak under his rule. At the same time, he made the empire easier to rule by improving the legal system, building roads, and setting up a universal currency.

BORN:	DIED:
550 BCE	486 BCE

This stone relief from Persepolis shows a group of ambassadors from Lydia carrying gifts for the Persian ruler.

THE END...AND THE BEGINNING

After the reign of Darius I's son, Xerxes I, ended in 465 BCE, the Achaemenid Empire became weaker. In 330 BCE, the Greek leader Alexander the Great (see pages 78–79) conquered Persepolis, and the Achaemenid Empire came to an end. But this was not the end of Persian culture. Two further empires eventually arose in this area: first the Parthian Empire from 247 BCE–224 CE and then the Sassanian Empire from 224–651 CE. This final Persian empire was eventually conquered by Muslim forces from Arabia.

The ruins of Persepolis still stand, including the Gate of All Nations (shown here), where people once arrived bearing tribute from all corners of the empire.

CENTRAL, SOUTHERN, AND EASTERN ASIA

STEPPE NOMADS
pp60–63

Asia is absolutely vast—it makes up about 30 percent of Earth's land area and is home to nearly 60 percent of the world's population. Modern humans may have reached Southeast Asia as far back as 50,000 years ago. Today, the continent encompasses a vast range of cultures, who speak about 2,300 different languages.

GUPTA EMPIRE
p49

KHMER EMPIRE
pp58–59

INDUS VALLEY
pp44–47

MAURYAN EMPIRE
p48

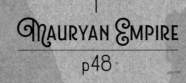

Bronze statue from the Indus Valley (see page 45)

Angkor Wat (see page 58)

This map identifies areas within the civilizations and cultures featured in this chapter. Turn to the listed pages to see their full extent.

Intricate goldwork from Silla (page 56)

Korean bronze bell (see page 57)

Ancient Korea
p56

Ancient China
pp50–55

Ancient Japan
p57

Chinese oracle bone (see page 54)

A Varied Continent

The landscapes of Asia include towering snow-capped mountains, vast deserts, dense forests, fertile river valleys, and coastal mangrove swamps. Although the distances are huge, people have been traveling across Asia for centuries to trade and settle. This fascinating land is the birthplace of many of the world's major religions, including Buddhism and Hinduism. They spread around the world, along with trade goods and new ideas and inventions.

INDUS VALLEY CIVILIZATIONS

The mighty Indus River travels more than 1,800 miles (3,000 km) on its journey from its source in the Himalayas, all the way to the Arabian Sea. Downstream, it carves out a valley where thousands of years ago, a sophisticated civilization developed. It thrived for many centuries before disappearing.

WHO LIVED HERE?

Thanks to the Indus River's annual flooding, people were able to live and farm along its banks from at least 7000 BCE. They lived in small villages at first, but gradually larger towns and cities began to appear. The people farmed wheat, barley, and cotton, and they domesticated animals such as dogs, goats, sheep, and cattle. By about 2600 BCE, there was an organized civilization marked by large cities.

The ruins of Harappa

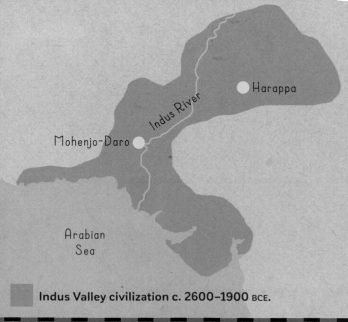

Indus Valley civilization c. 2600–1900 BCE.

HARAPPA

The city of Harappa was located toward the north of the Indus Valley region in what is now Pakistan. It was surrounded by defensive walls and arranged with a high central area where the important buildings were, and a lower city filled with homes and shops. This lower section was laid out in a grid pattern, showing that it was carefully planned. Homes had flat roofs that could be used as terraces. Larger homes were built around a courtyard. At its height, there may have been more than 40,000 people living there.

MOHENJO-DARO

Mohenjo-daro was situated farther downstream, about 600 km (370 miles) from Harappa. It had the same basic pattern as Harappa, as did other cities that have been discovered in the region. This is a clue that the Indus Valley civilization had a strong central government that could organize the building of cities. There are dockyards, warehouses, meeting rooms, and even a large public bath. Archaeologists think that Mohenjo-daro may have been the capital of the entire region.

Mohenjo-daro has some of the earliest known public baths, such as this complex from around 2500 BCE.

This bronze statue of a dancing girl was found in the ruins of Mohenjo-daro.

REDISCOVERY

The Indus Valley civilization may have been as large and advanced as that of Mesopotamia or Egypt, but for a long time no one really knew about it. After the civilization declined around 1800 BCE—for reasons that we still haven't figured out—the cities were abandoned. Their ruins were rediscovered by archaeologists in the 1800s. Since then, people have been trying to learn more about the people who lived there.

Writing

The people of the Indus Valley had a system of writing, which appeared on pottery, bones, bronze tools, and small tablets of various materials. It is also found on stamp seals, which could be pressed into wet clay to leave a shape or picture. The script includes more than 400 different symbols, but most of the inscriptions found so far are short, using just a handful of symbols. So far, no one has been able to decipher what they mean—we are not even sure what language they represent! This is one of the main reasons that we still know so little about the Indus Valley civilization.

Water

The Indus Valley people had a complex system for managing water. On their farmland, they used canals to irrigate their crops. Within their cities, they had wells to provide drinking water, and there was a system of terracotta pipes and sewers to take away dirty water. Some houses had toilets that were linked to the covered drains, creating the first-known indoor toilets. These toilets could be flushed by pouring water down them. Sanitation systems on this level wouldn't be seen again until the time of the Romans.

An ancient Indus Valley well close to the site of Harappa

This statue may show one of the priest-king rulers of Mohenjo-daro.

This terracotta seal from Harappa shows some Indus Valley script.

TRADE AND CONFLICT

The artifacts found at sites such as Harappa and Mohenjo-daro show that the Indus Valley people must have traded with other groups beyond their borders. There are objects made of turquoise, alabaster and lapis lazuli from Iran, and gold and copper from other places. The Indus Valley people traded or bartered instead of using money. Archaeologists have found few weapons, and no evidence of an army or war damage to the buildings, so it looks as though the civilization was mostly peaceful.

INDUS VALLEY ART

The Indus Valley people made sculptures—usually showing human figures—out of clay, stone, and bronze. Many of these were probably used for religious worship. Archaeologists have also found clay toys, such as whistles, toy carts (below), and cattle that nod their heads. Women wore necklaces, bracelets, and earrings made from gold and silver as well as shells and semi-precious gemstones.

THE MAURYAN EMPIRE

The appearance of the Mauryan Empire during the early fourth century BCE marked the first time that India was united under one ruler. The empire stretched from the Arabian Sea in the west to the shores of the Bay of Bengal in the east.

THE MAURYAN EMPIRE

In 322 BCE, Chandragupta Maurya, ruler of the kingdom of Maghada in northeast India, began to expand westward—this was the start of the Mauryan Empire, which had its capital at the city of Pataliputra. Legends say that Chandragupta was very paranoid, never sleeping in the same bed twice. In about 298 BCE, Chandragupta abdicated to become a monk in the Jain religion, and the kingdom passed to his son, Bindusara.

Pataliputra
MAGHADA
KALINGA
Arabian Sea
Bay of Bengal

Mauryan Empire c. 250 BCE

ASHOKA'S RULE

Bindusara pushed the empire's borders farther south, and when he died in 273 BCE, his son Ashoka took over. Ashoka expanded the empire even more, taking over the kingdom of Kalinga after a long, bloody battle. Appalled by the violence, Ashoka converted to Buddhism and became a peaceful ruler. He encouraged his people to convert to Buddhism, building holy buildings called stupas, such as the one on the left. He died in about 232 BCE and the empire collapsed about fifty years later.

THE GUPTA EMPIRE

Some 500 years after the fall of the Mauryan empire, another power rose to unite most of India—the Gupta Empire. This empire would rule most of northern and southern India for nearly 250 years.

THE GUPTA EMPIRE

A new empire began in about 320 CE, and, just like the Mauryan Empire, its first leader was also called Chandragupta. His capital city was Pataliputra, which is also where the Mauryan emperors' capital had been. Thanks to a strong army, and marriage to the princess of a nearby kingdom, Chandragupta and his descendants expanded the empire across the subcontinent.

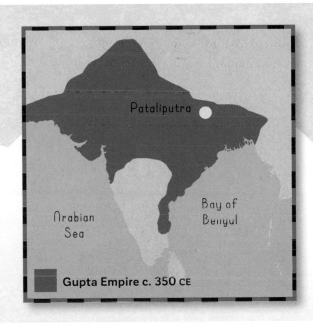

Pataliputra

Arabian Sea

Bay of Bengal

Gupta Empire c. 350 CE

A GOLDEN AGE

A Gupta sculpture showing the god Vishnu

The Gupta Empire lasted until 550 CE, and it was a largely peaceful time. Traders sold cotton, spices, gemstones, steel, and fine cashmere wool to customers in Europe, Africa, and China, bringing wealth into the empire. Peace and prosperity during the Gupta period meant that arts and learning could flourish. Literature from this period, written in the Sanskrit language, has survived. Scholars such as the mathematician and astronomer Aryabhata made advances in the sciences. In the middle of the sixth century CE, invasions by peoples from Central Asia brought the empire to an end.

ANCIENT CHINA

In Western Asia, it was the cultivation of wheat and barley that led to the first civilizations. But in East Asia, the beginning of farming involved a different crop—rice. It would become the backbone of one of the world's great civilizations—China.

THE SHANG DYNASTY

By the second millennium BCE, much of China was ruled by powerful families who passed the throne down from one member to another—this is called a dynasty. One of the earliest examples was the Shang Dynasty. According to Chinese historical tradition, the Shang came to power in about 1600 BCE under a leader called Tang, and their rule would last for more than 500 years. Tang wanted to rule for the good of the people, and he created government programs to help the poor. The Shang ruled a large area of what is now northeast China from their capital at Yin (now known as Anyang).

The Shang Dynasty marked the beginning of the Bronze Age in China (see pages 14–15). Skilled craftworkers made beautiful cups and bowls out of bronze.

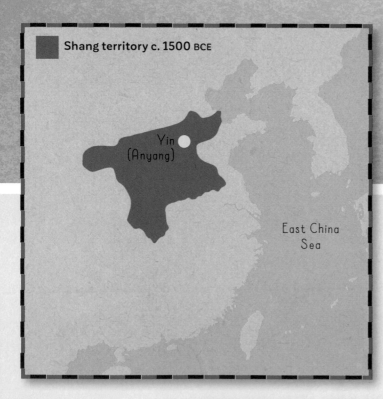

Shang territory c. 1500 BCE

Yin (Anyang)

East China Sea

THE ZHOU

The Shang Dynasty came to an end in 1046 BCE when its emperor was defeated in battle by King Wu. His victory marked the start of the Zhou Dynasty. Like rulers during the Shang Dynasty, the Zhou rulers believed that the gods had given them the right to rule over the people. They gave land to nobles who owed them a debt of loyalty. The nobles also paid taxes and provided soldiers when needed. Peasants worked the land for the nobles.

NEW RELIGIONS

The Zhou Dynasty lasted for more than 700 years, and two new philosophies arose during that time. One was Daoism (sometimes spelled Taoism), which arose from the teachings of a man named Lao Tzu. It emphasizes living in harmony with nature, in accordance with a cosmic force called the Dao, which flows through all things. The second philosophy is Confucianism, which encourages people to live a moral life. Both philosophies became a way of life for many people.

Lao Tzu wrote a book of poetry called the *Daodejing* to describe his ideas about living at peace with the world.

King Wu only ruled for about three years before his death. The throne passed to his son Cheng.

CONFUCIUS

Confucius lived from 551–479 BCE, in the state of Lu, where he worked for the local ruler. Later, he started a school in his hometown and wrote down his ideas. Confucius believed that people are essentially good, and that having good moral character led to peace and harmony. Bad things, such as natural disasters, were the result of not following the ancient teachings.

A statue of Confucius

BORN:	DIED:
551 BCE	479 BCE

THE WARRING STATES

The Chu and the Qin states occupied the largest territories during the Warring States period in around 260 BCE.

By about 481 BCE, the Zhou kings were in trouble. Their system of ruling over semi-independent nobles was crumbling. Their territory split into about 100 small states, each ruled over by a local leader. These small states often fought, giving this era its name—the Warring States period. Huge battles with bronze weapons ended up with powerful states taking over smaller ones, and eventually there were only seven left. The two most powerful states were known as the Chu and the Qin.

THE FIRST EMPEROR

The situation was ripe for a powerful leader to unite the states and unify China. This man was King Zheng, ruler of the Qin. After several years and many battles, he succeeded in defeating the last of the other states in 221 BCE. For the first time, China was unified under a single emperor. Zheng took the name Qin Shi Huang which means "Qin first emperor." He got rid of his rivals and drafted hundreds of thousands of people to serve in the army or on his building projects.

Qin Shi Huang died in 210 BCE and the empire collapsed just a few years later.

ONE RULER, ONE CHINA

Qin Shi Huang was a brutal but effective ruler. He set up a capital in the city of Xianyang and started organizing his empire. He set up a new currency and a system of weights and measures that everyone had to use. He also ordered that different writing systems be consolidated, so that all of China's languages could be written down with the same set of characters. He commissioned a series of border defenses stretching nearly 3,000 miles (5,000 km). These earthen barriers formed a "Great Wall."

Little remains of Qin Shi Huang's great wall but it inspired the Ming dynasty to build their own stone and brick Great Wall over 1,500 years later.

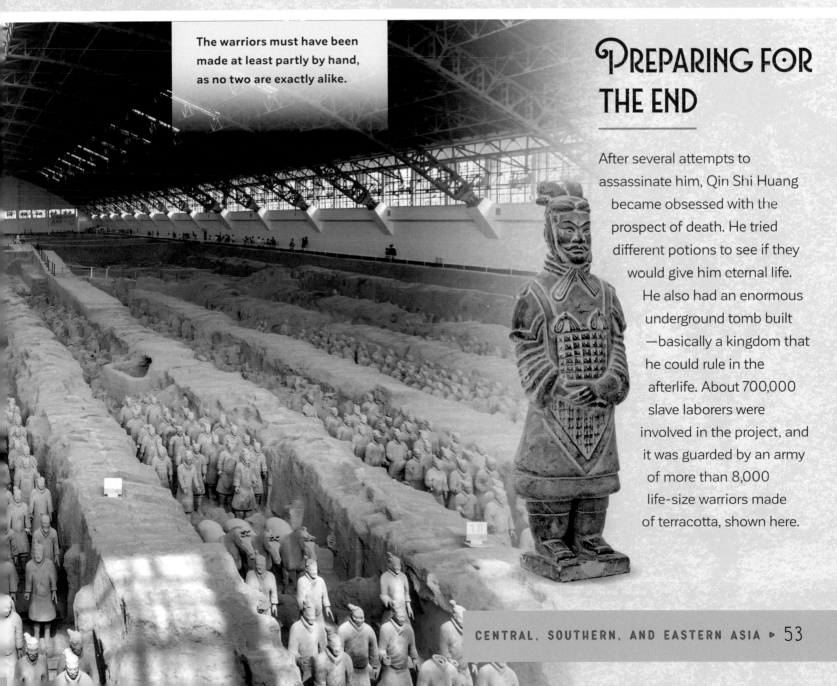

The warriors must have been made at least partly by hand, as no two are exactly alike.

PREPARING FOR THE END

After several attempts to assassinate him, Qin Shi Huang became obsessed with the prospect of death. He tried different potions to see if they would give him eternal life. He also had an enormous underground tomb built —basically a kingdom that he could rule in the afterlife. About 700,000 slave laborers were involved in the project, and it was guarded by an army of more than 8,000 life-size warriors made of terracotta, shown here.

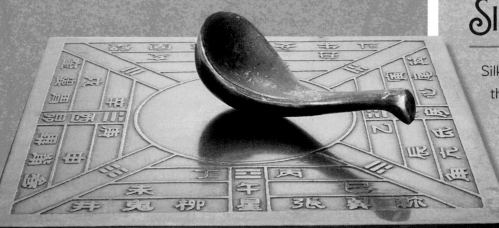

Early Chinese compasses were used originally for fortune telling and only later for navigation.

SILK

Silk is a natural fiber produced by the larvae of the silkworm moth, which use it to make their cocoons. People in China began raising silkworms and weaving the silk fibers into cloth in about 3600 BCE. But it was later, during the Shang and Zhou Dynasties, that they began to produce beautiful silk fabrics on a large scale. This became one of the most important goods that the Chinese traded with other peoples. Archaeologists have found examples of Shang-era silk in an Egyptian tomb. The Chinese were able to keep the process of silk making secret for thousands of years, until two monks managed to smuggle silkworm eggs back to Constantinople in 552 CE.

LEAVING THEIR MARK

Many rulers during the Shang and Zhou periods wanted to improve life for their people, and this often meant new ways of thinking and doing things. Healers used acupuncture and herbal remedies to keep people healthy. Astronomers tracked the stars and planets—mainly to make predictions about the future, but also to keep careful records of comets, sunspots, and other space events. This was also a time of new inventions, including kites and magnetic compasses, that would go on to change the world.

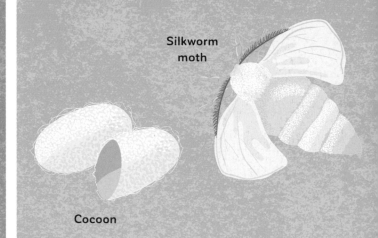

Silkworm moth

Cocoon

Once an oracle bone had cracked, the diviner would interpret the cracks to reveal an answer.

WRITING

Chinese writing began during the Shang Dynasty with the use of oracle bones. When someone had a big decision to make, they would go to a person called a diviner, who carved symbols onto an animal bone and then heated it until it cracked. These simple markings evolved into a type of writing, with symbols representing objects or ideas. They were carved on wood or bronze, or written on bamboo scrolls.

IRON

The Chinese were not the first people to use iron, but they were the first to develop a new form called cast iron. Other cultures heated iron until it was soft and then hammered it into shape. Using bellows, Chinese metalworkers were able to heat it enough so that it melted completely. It could then be poured into a shaped mold and allowed to cool and harden. They used this technique to make weapons, tools, and other objects, such as the bowl on the left.

A Chinese cast-iron bowl at a temple made in about 300 CE

PAPER

The Chinese developed the first true paper some time during the Eastern Han period (25–220 CE). Before then, texts were written on bone or bamboo tablets. The earliest processes involved soaking rags and plant fibers to form a pulp, which was then squeezed to remove the water and dried to form thin sheets. Later, in around 700, the Chinese would become the first civlization to develop printing, using wooden blocks.

Made in 868 BCE, this is a paper page from the oldest dated printed book in the world.

ANCIENT KOREA

The oldest settlements found in Korea date back to about 6000 BCE. A few thousand years later, people in Korea began to grow rice and to build imposing stone tombs called *goindols*, many of which are still standing today. Because Korea is so close to China, the culture here was heavily influenced by ideas and innovations from China.

GOJOSEON

The first large-scale kingdom in Korea was Gojoseon (sometimes written as Old Chosun). Legend says that it was founded in 2333 BCE by a king named Dangun, though many historians think that it probably began much later. With the help of iron tools introduced from China, farming improved and the kingdom thrived. This period is known for gray stoneware pottery and for underfloor heating called *ondol*, which used a fire to warm an underfloor cavity.

More than 30,000 tombs like this still stand in Korea.

THREE KINGDOMS

Gojoseon collapsed in around 194 BCE, after many years of attacks from neighboring groups. Then in 108 BCE, China invaded and took over. But before long, three Korean kingdoms emerged —Goguryeo, Paekche, and Silla —pushing the Chinese back. These kingdoms sometimes cooperated and sometimes fought. At first, Goguryeo was the largest and most powerful, but Silla slowly rose until it conquered the others in 668 CE.

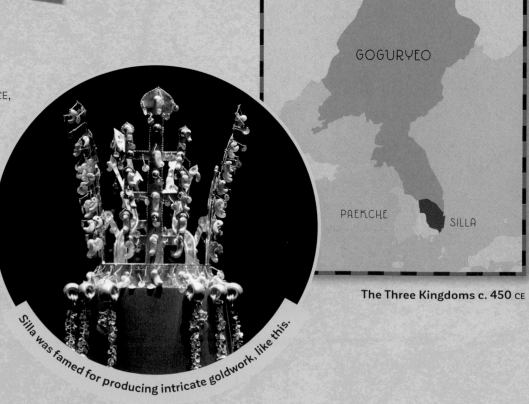

Silla was famed for producing intricate goldwork, like this.

GOGURYEO

PAEKCHE

SILLA

The Three Kingdoms c. 450 CE

ANCIENT JAPAN

The islands of Japan were settled later than China and Korea. The first Japanese culture that we know of is called the *Jōmon*. This name means "rope patterned," and it comes from the pottery produced during this time, which had patterns pressed into the clay before firing. Jōmon pottery is some of the oldest in the world, dating from around 10,000 BCE. The Jōmon people were hunter-gatherers at first, but they had begun farming by around 5000 BCE.

An example of a Jōmon vessel (above) and a close-up of the rope pattern made on a Jōmon pot (left)

THE YAYOI CULTURE

The era from about 300 BCE to 250 CE in Japan is known as the Yayoi Period. During this time, immigrants arrived from Korea and they brought new techniques in pottery, metalworking, and weaving. Thanks to other advances, farming improved and the Yayoi society developed. Local chiefs ruled over their villages, but there was no large-scale kingdom.

Bronze bells like this one from the 1st–2nd centuries CE were used in Yayoi religious rituals.

THE YAMATO PERIOD

By about 250 CE, one of the regional clans—the Yamato—had become dominant and would unite Japan under one ruler for the first time. The period is also called the Kofun period, after the giant burial mounds that were built at this time for important people. During this period, Japanese civilization was heavily influenced by Chinese religion, writing, and political ideas. But from the 9th century onward, a more distinctly Japanese culture emerged.

It would have taken the work of many laborers to build huge, elaborate burial mounds like this.

THE KHMER EMPIRE

We know relatively little about the peoples who lived in southeast Asia in ancient times. Once writing was introduced sometime after 200 CE, the picture becomes a bit clearer. Then, around the year 800 CE, a young prince named Jayavarman laid the foundations for what would become the mighty Khmer Empire.

BUILDING AN EMPIRE

From their capital city of Angkor in what is now Cambodia, the Khmer gradually expanded their territory. At its height, the Khmer Empire reached from modern-day Myanmar east to Vietnam, and north into southern China. Some of its kings were Hindu, while others were Buddhist.

A view of the main temple complex at Angkor Wat

The Khmer Empire was an organized state that conducted regular counts of the population, called censuses. Travelers who visited the empire from China were often surprised that most of the buying and selling of goods in the marketplaces was done by women, which was unusual at the time in many parts of the world.

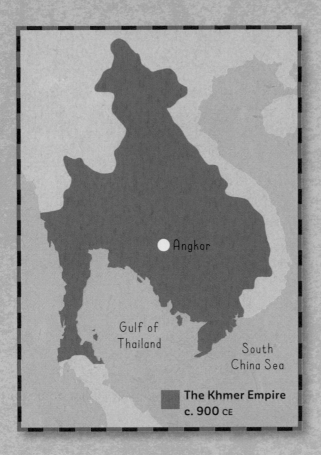

Angkor

Gulf of Thailand

South China Sea

The Khmer Empire c. 900 CE

KHMER ENGINEERING

Southeast Asia receives heavy rain as part of the monsoon season, flooding rivers and lakes, but is very dry at other times. The Khmer developed systems to collect and store water, diverting rivers and digging canals to link huge reservoirs. People and goods traveled along the canals through different parts of the empire. Many of the bridges built over the canals had tall, narrow arches that could be blocked to control how much water passed through. The reservoirs could hold water to prevent flooding during the monsoon, and this water could be used to irrigate crops during the dry season.

ANGKOR WAT

As well as building canals and bridges, the Khmer also built temples and palaces. The temple complex at Angkor Wat is the most famous. Surrounded by a moat, it covers an area of 0.7 sq miles (2 sq km), making it one of the world's largest religious structures, and took about 30 years to build. It was commissioned by the emperor Suryavarman II in the early 1100s as a way of showing his devotion to the Hindu god Vishnu. The temple is designed to represent Mount Meru, which in Hinduism is the center of the universe. After the Khmer Empire collapsed in 1431, the temple was reclaimed by the thick jungle and only restored in the 1800s.

Large reservoirs, such as this one at Angkor Wat, were used for bathing or to irrigate crops.

STEPPE NOMADS

A civilization is usually marked by cities and impressive buildings. But to do that, you need to stay in one place. In the vast grasslands, or steppes, of Asia, several powerful groups emerged from about 1300 BCE, and although they had a complicated culture, they were not civilizations in the strict sense. They were nomads, living their life on the move and using horses to get around.

CIMMERIANS AND SCYTHIANS

The Cimmerians originated in an area bordered by the Black Sea, the Caucasus Mountains, and the Caspian Sea—land that is now part of southern Russia. Sometime around the 700s BCE, they were pushed south from their homeland into what is now Iran. The people doing the pushing were a related group called the Scythians. The Scythians were renowned in the ancient world as being fierce warriors, and they would eventually dominate the steppes of western Asia.

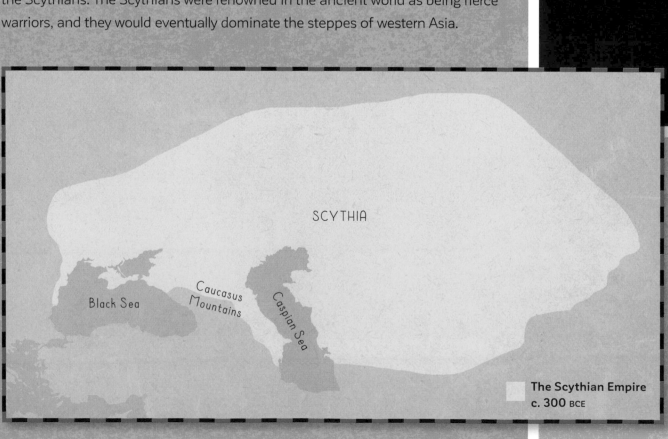

SCYTHIA

Black Sea

Caucasus Mountains

Caspian Sea

The Scythian Empire
c. 300 BCE

Good as Gold

Most of the examples of Scythian art that archaeologists have found were small and portable. The Scythians were known for the fine quality of their gold work. Even everyday items like combs and drinking cups could be made from gold with elaborate decorations, often showing scenes of Scythian life. The gold was often inlaid with glass or gemstones. Many pieces have holes so they could be sewn onto clothing, belts, or harnesses.

This Scythian golden pectoral (necklace) was discovered in a burial mound and dates from around the fourth century BCE.

Ateas

Roman and Greek historians wrote about the Scythian king Ateas, though little is known about his life. He expanded the Scythian territory into Thrace. This brought him into conflict with the powerful Macedonians, and in 339 BCE Ateas was killed in battle at the age of 90 while fighting the army of Philip II of Macedon—the father of Alexander the Great (see pages 78–79).

BORN·	DIED·
c. 429 BCE	339 BCE

Life on Horseback

The grass of the steppes provided food for the Scythians' horses, as well as for their herds of cattle and sheep. When on the move, they pulled covered wagons that served as portable homes. The Scythians didn't use stirrups, but they did use saddles, bridles, and bits. They also developed a bow made from different layers of material, which was more powerful than a plain wooden bow. A group of Scythian archers on horseback could use their bows to shoot a barrage of bronze-tipped arrows that could pierce armor.

A modern replica of Scythian horse headgear

WHAT'S LEFT?

The Scythians didn't leave behind grand buildings and they had no written language, so much of what we know about them comes from writers from other cultures —and it may or may not be true. The Scythians did build large burial mounds called kurgans (right). In them, archaeologists have found mummified bodies that were covered in tattoos. The mummies were buried alongside goods for the afterlife including bowls, cups, carpets, and even horses in elaborate costumes. By the 2nd century BCE, the Scythians had been absorbed by other kingdoms.

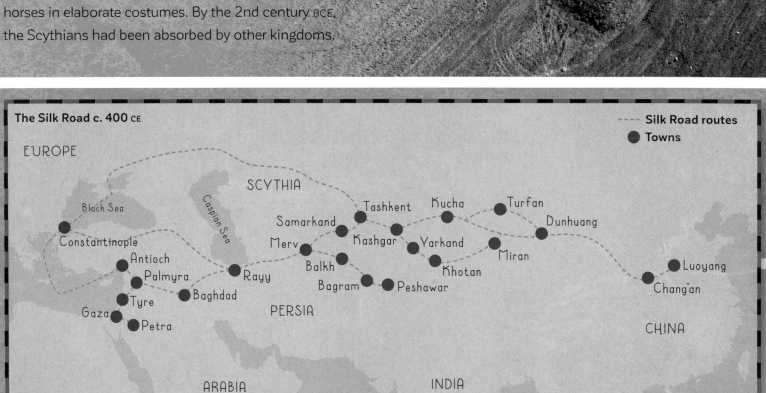

The Silk Road c. 400 CE

- - - - Silk Road routes
● Towns

EUROPE

Black Sea

Constantinople

Antioch
Palmyra
Tyre
Gaza
Petra

Baghdad

Caspian Sea

Rayy

SCYTHIA

Merv
Balkh

Samarkand
Kashgar

Tashkent

Kucha

Turfan

Dunhuang

Yarkand
Khotan

Miran

Bagram   Peshawar

PERSIA

ARABIA

INDIA

Luoyang
Chang'an

CHINA

THE SILK ROAD

The Scythian territory overlapped with part of an ancient trading route known as the Silk Road. The Silk Road wasn't a single paved highway—it was a network of different routes traveled by traders who often used pack animals such as camels to carry the goods. Starting in around 130 BCE, this route linked China with Europe and western Asia. Few people traveled the entire route, which was more than 3,700 miles (6,000 km) long. A merchant would carry his goods for part of the way, then trade them with another merchant who would take them farther and then exchange again, and so on.

THE MONGOLS

Traveling the Silk Road could be dangerous. Rugged terrain and harsh weather were one problem, and the tribes of nomadic raiders that lived along the route were another. Ironically, one of these nomadic tribes would end up bringing peace to the Silk Road. Long after the Scythians had disappeared, the Mongols united under the leadership of Genghis Khan. With a fearsome army of horsemen, he conquered vast areas of Asia and founded the Mongol Empire in 1206. With large parts of the Silk Road under one rule, it became safer to travel, which lasted until the growth of the Ottoman Empire in the 15th century cut the land trade between East and West.

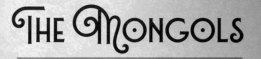

A statue of Genghis Khan built on the plains outside Ulaanbaatar, Mongolia

SILK ROAD GOODS

Historians in the 19th century gave these routes the name "the Silk Road" because this is how silk from China reached Europe. But many other goods were traded as well. Horses, furs, grapevines, glassware, textiles, camels, slaves, and precious metals were sent from west to east. In return, goods such as ivory, tea, precious stones, porcelain, spices, and rice made their way to the west. In addition to physical goods, new ideas and technology were carried as well. For example, Buddhism arrived in China from India via the Silk Road, and Chinese inventions such as paper and gunpowder were carried westward.

This statue from Samarkand, Uzbekistan, shows a group of traders about to set off along the Silk Road.

Solar chariot
(see page 91)

Viking Ancestors

Celts

Romulus
and Remus
(see page 80)

Germanic Tribes

Ancient Rome

This map identifies areas
within civilizations
featured in this chapter.
Turn to the listed pages to
see their full extent and to
find out more about them.

Mycenae

EUROPE

Europe may be one of the smallest continents, and it wasn't the first to be settled, but it has been a major influence on our modern world and culture. Yet in ancient times, most of Europe beyond the Mediterranean region was considered to be on the fringes of the civilized world.

Alexander the Great (see page 78)

MACEDON & ALEXANDER THE GREAT)
pp78–79

Sappho
(see page 77)

ANCIENT GREECE
pp72–77

MINOANS
pp68–69

NORTH AND SOUTH

The earliest large-scale civilizations in Europe grew along the Mediterranean coast, where they could trade with other peoples in Africa and western Asia. This level of organization only came later in northern Europe, thanks in part to a cooler climate that was less suited to farming. The people of northern Europe were often dismissed as "barbarians" by the Greeks and Romans, but before long their civilizations became just as advanced.

STONE AGE EUROPE

Until about 11,000 years ago, much of northern Europe was covered in a sheet of ice. As Earth's climate warmed and the ice receded, people moved into the new land. These people mainly lived as hunter-gatherers, using simple stone tools. The remains they left behind provide tantalizing clues about what life was like.

EARLY SITES

At Carnac, in the French region of Brittany, more than 3,000 standing stones stretch in rows across the land. The smallest stones are less than a yard tall, while the largest stand over 21.5 ft (6.5 m). Some are placed on top of two upright stones to form tomb entrances. But others stand on their own, and historians aren't sure what their purpose was. In Ireland, the site of Newgrange is home to a huge tomb, with passages and chambers hidden beneath an earthen mound. It was built around 3200 BCE, about the same time as the later stones at Carnac were being erected.

The standing stones at Carnac, France

The large tomb at Newgrange, Ireland

Art and Artifacts

Soon bronze technology was introduced throughout Europe. Archaeologists have found many artifacts from this period. They include four-wheeled wagons as well as miniature bronze models of wheeled carts and chariots. There are also swords, bowls and cauldrons, and jewelry such as necklaces, brooches, and pendants. Many artifacts were found buried together in what is called a hoard. They may have been put in the ground as gifts for the gods.

A bronze toy chariot from around 1300 BCE found at Dupljaja, Serbia

The Urnfield Culture

By about 1300 BCE, a new culture began to spread out from central Europe. It has been called the Urnfield culture because these people cremated their dead, then buried the ashes in clay urns. They built walled settlements on hilltops and left behind pottery, bronze tools, and armor. The culture eventually spread as far as Spain in the west and Ukraine in the east.

Stonehenge

Stonehenge, which stands on England's Salisbury Plain, is one of the most famous prehistoric European monuments. It was built in different stages between 3000 BCE and 1520 BCE, and it consists of a circle of huge standing stones with horizontal stones placed across the top, as well as many smaller surrounding stones and burial mounds. The stones are precisely aligned to the position of the Sun at the winter and summer solstices, so the site was probably used for ceremonies of some sort.

The fallen bluestones shown in this image of Stonehenge are from Wales—about 185 miles (300 km) away—and weigh several tons. No one is quite sure how they were moved to their current position.

MINOANS

The first advanced civilization in

Europe arose on the Greek island of Crete about 5,000 years ago. These Bronze Age people were called the Minoans, and their culture spread around the Aegean Sea before later collapsing around 1100 BCE.

PALACES

Around 2000 BCE, the Minoans began to build large palaces. These complexes were several stories high and had courtyards, storerooms, underground crypts, drainage systems, and even theater areas. The walls were decorated with brightly colored wall paintings called frescoes, such as the one below. Four major palaces have been found, and the largest of all is Knossos. The palaces were destroyed in around 1700 BCE, probably by an earthquake. They were rebuilt but then destroyed again in around 1450 BCE by an invasion, which brought the civilization to an end.

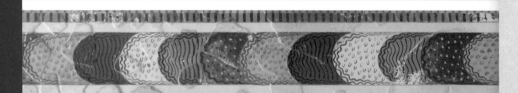

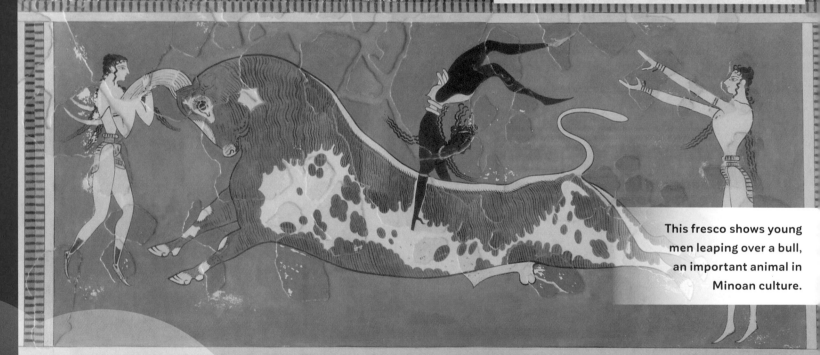

This fresco shows young men leaping over a bull, an important animal in Minoan culture.

TRAVEL AND TRADE

The Minoans raised animals and grew crops such as wheat, grapes, olives, and figs. They were also good sailors, and they built roads to get these crops to ports on the coast, and then shipped them around the eastern Mediterranean. Goods from Crete have been found in mainland Greece, Turkey, and Egypt. In return, the Minoans received raw materials, such as bronze, as well as new ideas and technologies.

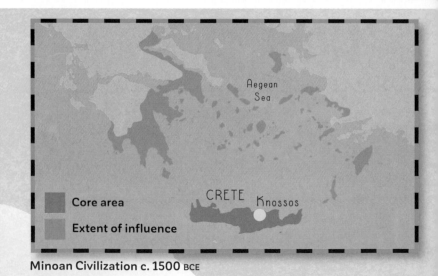

Aegean Sea

Core area

Extent of influence

CRETE Knossos

Minoan Civilization c. 1500 BCE

The mythical Minotaur was killed by the Greek hero Theseus.

MYTHS AND LEGENDS

Later Greek myths told of a king of Crete named Minos. After winning a war against the city-state of Athens, he demanded that every nine years, Athens send young men and women. They would be eaten by the Minotaur, a beast with the head of a bull who lived in a labyrinth. The story is made up, but there may possibly have been a real King Minos who lived in one of the Minoan palaces. And the Minoans considered bulls to be sacred animals, which might be the source of the myth of the Minotaur.

REDISCOVERY

The civilization was rediscovered in 1900 by the British archaeologist Sir Arthur Evans, who took the name "Minoan" from the legendary King Minos, because the many rooms of the palace at Knossos reminded him of the labyrinth from Greek myth. Evans excavated the site for 35 years and made many discoveries, including a writing system that he called Linear A. It has never been deciphered.

Evans reconstructed some of the remains at Knossos as they might once have looked.

MYCENAEANS

If the collapse of the Minoan civilization really was due to an invasion (see pages 68–69), then it's likely that the invaders were the Mycenaeans. This civilization had its start on the Greek mainland, but they ruled over many of the nearby islands and traded with other groups across the Mediterranean.

People and goods entered the walled city of Mycenae through this gate, guarded by stone lions.

PALACES AND TOMBS

Starting in about 1700 BCE, the Mycenaeans began to build large walled palaces and citadels. It is believed that each one of these hilltop strongholds controlled a small kingdom. Mycenae was the largest, but there were more than 100 others, including Tiryns, Pylos, and Thebes. At these settlements, the Mycenaeans also built stone *tholos* tombs, which were dome-shaped and looked a bit like beehives. These kingdoms shared the same architecture, painting and pottery styles, weapons, and language—a script known as Linear B, which is the oldest form of written Greek.

SHIPS AND TRADE

At first, the Mycenaeans were influenced by Minoan culture, and the two civilizations existed side-by-side. But after the collapse of the Minoans, the Mycenaeans became the dominant group in the Aegean. Their ships sailed around the Mediterranean, carrying pottery, olive oil and wine to trade for gold, ivory, and other materials. Archaeologists have found a shipwreck from around 1330 BCE. It was likely on its way to a Mycenaean port, carrying a cargo of raw metals, glass, arrowheads, nuts and fruits, and even hippopotamus teeth!

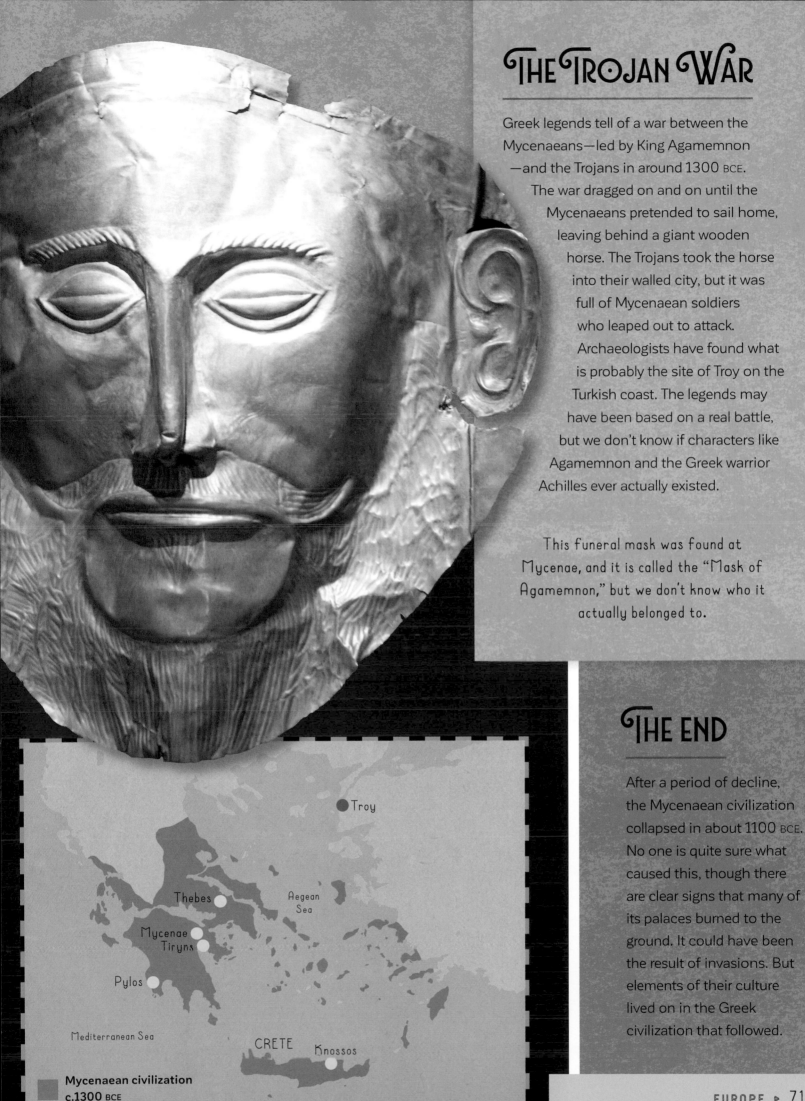

THE TROJAN WAR

Greek legends tell of a war between the Mycenaeans—led by King Agamemnon—and the Trojans in around 1300 BCE. The war dragged on and on until the Mycenaeans pretended to sail home, leaving behind a giant wooden horse. The Trojans took the horse into their walled city, but it was full of Mycenaean soldiers who leaped out to attack. Archaeologists have found what is probably the site of Troy on the Turkish coast. The legends may have been based on a real battle, but we don't know if characters like Agamemnon and the Greek warrior Achilles ever actually existed.

This funeral mask was found at Mycenae, and it is called the "Mask of Agamemnon," but we don't know who it actually belonged to.

THE END

After a period of decline, the Mycenaean civilization collapsed in about 1100 BCE. No one is quite sure what caused this, though there are clear signs that many of its palaces burned to the ground. It could have been the result of invasions. But elements of their culture lived on in the Greek civilization that followed.

Troy

Thebes

Aegean Sea

Mycenae
Tiryns

Pylos

Mediterranean Sea

CRETE
Knossos

Mycenaean civilization
c.1300 BCE

ANCIENT GREECE

After the fall of the Mycenaeans (see pages 70–71), Greece fell into a period of decline often called the "Dark Age." The population shrank and the settlements were mainly small and scattered. But in about 800 BCE, some of these settlements started to grow into powerful city-states. They would be at the heart of a Greek golden age that would last for centuries.

CITY-STATES

In ancient times, Greece was not a unified country like it is today. Instead, it was made up of many independent city-states—called *poleis* in Greek—each consisting of a city and the countryside around it. The upper part of a city, called the acropolis, was often surrounded by walls and was the location of temples, palaces, and forts. The lower city, usually also surrounded by a defensive wall, was where ordinary people lived, worked, and shopped. Greek city-states sometimes fought with each other, but at other times they banded together to fight a common enemy, such as the Persians.

You can still see temples and other public buildings at the Acropolis in Athens.

SPREADING OUT

As the city-states and their populations grew, they needed more land and more resources. Starting in around 800 BCE, they began to set up colonies across the Mediterranean. They would start by establishing trade links with a new area, then send settlers to build cities. In this way, Greek culture and language spread across the region, and eventually there were about 500 Greek colonies in places as far afield as modern-day France, Libya, Egypt, Turkey, and Ukraine. By 500 BCE, about 40 percent of all Greeks lived outside of Greece.

EUROPE

Antipolis

Istros

Theodosia

Black Sea

Phasis

Byzantion

Sinope

Neapolis

Heraclea

Thebes

Corinth

Athens

Selinus

Syracuse

Sparta

Mediterranean Sea

Paphos

AFRICA

Cyrene

Area of Greek influence c. 500 BCE

Greek cities and colonies were scattered across the Mediterranean.

RELIGION AND BELIEFS

One aspect of Greek culture that spread with the colonies was their religion. The Greeks believed in a pantheon, or group, of gods and goddesses. The gods—who were all related to each other in some way—looked like humans, and they acted like humans too, falling in love, having children, and often quarrelling. Each one controlled an aspect of the world and/or daily life. For example, Poseidon was the god of the sea and Demeter was the goddess of the harvest. People prayed to the gods and left offerings and sacrifices at temples in order to keep them happy.

Zeus was the god of the sky and thunder as well as king of all the gods. Like other gods, he sometimes disguised himself and walked among mortals.

Athens

The history of Athens goes back to the Mycenaeans. After their collapse, it grew from a small settlement to be one of the most powerful city-states in Greece. The land surrounding it wasn't ideal for farming, so Athens depended on trade by ship, through its port at Piraeus. The city-state had a strong army and navy that won many battles, but the city was also home to great thinkers, writers, and artists.

Sparta

One of Athens' main rivals was Sparta. The Spartans had a very different outlook from the other Greek city-states. Military strength was most important to them, and they were famous for their tough fighters. Everyone had to keep fit and healthy, and all boys were trained to fight before eventually joining the army.

Spartan girls were encouraged to be fit and took part in running races, as shown in this bronze decoration. They had more rights in Sparta than elsewhere.

Weapons and War

With their long hair and red cloaks, Spartan soldiers were some of the most feared in the ancient world. They largely used the same weapons and armor as soldiers from other Greek city-states. These foot soldiers, known as hoplites, wore armor of stiffened linen or bronze and carried shields, spears, and swords with iron blades.

Statue of a Spartan hoplite from around 480 BCE

Athens was named for Athena, the goddess of wisdom and warfare. Her head appears on one side of this Athenian coin from the 4th century BCE, and an owl (one of her symbols) on the other.

DEMOCRACY

For a long time, Athens was ruled by small groups of rich landowners. Then in 508 BCE, a man named Cleisthenes introduced a new political system called democracy where people got to vote on how to run the city. However, women, slaves, and any man who was not an official citizen could not vote.

A bust of Cleisthenes

These tokens were used by ancient Greeks to cast their votes.

Remains of the paved trackway in Corinth across which whole warships could be carried

SHIPPING AND TRADE

The Greeks had fast, agile warships powered by sails and multiple banks of rowers. They also had cargo ships for trading across the Mediterranean. The Greeks exported wine, olives, and pottery in return for goods such as gold, copper, grains, spices, and glass.

CORINTH

The southern part of Greece is connected to the rest of the mainland by a thin strip of land known as an isthmus. Corinth's position on this isthmus made it an important port and naval base. Its people built a paved trackway that ran about 4.5 miles (7 km) from the port on one side to a second port on the other. To save ships a long and dangerous journey around the southern peninsula, goods could be hauled across.

Traded right across the Mediterranean, Greek pottery was often decorated with scenes from myths and legends.

GREEK ART

Over the centuries, Greek art and architecture became increasingly sophisticated. Buildings like temples were constructed according to strict mathematical rules, to make sure that all their parts were in proportion. Roofs were held up by tall columns with carved tops called capitals. The Greeks also carved statues from stone, showing the human body in an idealistic and beautiful way. These sculptures were so popular that the Romans later had copies made to put on display.

A Roman copy of an ancient Greek statue from around 460 BCE showing a discus thrower

DRAMA

The Greeks wrote and performed plays that are still staged today. People flocked to outdoor amphitheaters to watch tragedies about heroes and legends, or comedies that mocked politicians. Actors wearing masks would speak the dialogue, while a group of performers, known as a chorus, would together act as the narrator. This kind of performance had its roots in religious rituals to honor the gods—just like the sporting competition of the Olympic Games.

PHILOSOPHY

Greek thinkers liked nothing more than to ponder the big questions about the world around them. Our word "philosophy" comes from the Greek, meaning "a love of wisdom." The philosophers of Greece wanted to figure out how the world works and how best to live their lives. Thinkers such as Plato (c. 425–c. 347 BCE), Socrates (c. 470–399 BCE), and Epicurus (341–270 BCE) discussed their ideas with their followers and wrote them down — including many works that have survived.

Greek philosophers in Athens as imagined by the Italian painter Raphael between 1509 and 1511.

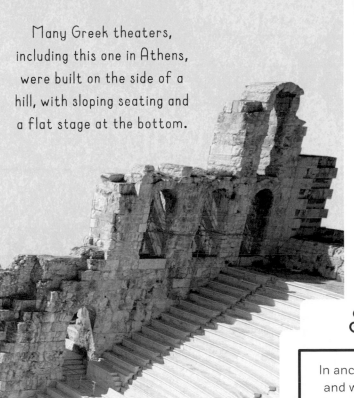

Many Greek theaters, including this one in Athens, were built on the side of a hill, with sloping seating and a flat stage at the bottom.

SCIENCE AND MATH

The Greeks made great advances in the fields of science, medicine, and mathematics. A doctor named Hippocrates (c. 460–c. 370 BCE) was one of the first to teach that illnesses had natural causes rather than being sent by the gods. The philosopher Aristotle (384–322 BCE) wrote widely about the natural world. Mathematicians such as Euclid (fl. c. 300 BCE) and Pythagoras (c. 570–c. 495 BCE) developed new ways of thinking about math, and used logic to prove their theories.

SAPPHO

In ancient Greece, women had few rights and were expected to stay in the home. Only a handful, such as the poet Sappho, got a chance to leave their mark. She lived from about 610–570 BCE, on the island of Lesbos, and wrote beautiful love poetry. It would have been performed aloud, accompanied by music on a lyre.

BORN:	DIED:
c. 610 BCE	c. 570 BCE

ALEXANDER'S EMPIRE

At the end of the 4th century BCE, Greece was swallowed up by a new power that quickly built up a huge empire but collapsed not long after. The Macedonian empire was a bit like a meteor —burning fast and brightly before fizzling out.

Philip II

Philip II became king of Macedon in 359 BCE. This kingdom was Greece's neighbor to the north, and most Greeks thought it was full of uncultured barbarians. But Philip reorganized its army, and as his power grew, the Greek city-states began to get very nervous. Through battles and diplomacy, Philip expanded his territory and, in 338 BCE, he won a large victory and took control of most of Greece. His next plan was to invade Persia, but he was assassinated in 336 BCE before he could begin.

A marble bust of Philip, who was murdered by a bodyguard. The assassin might have been working for the Persians or even for Philip's wife Olympias.

Alexander the Great

The throne passed to Philip's son Alexander, who was only 20 years old but already an experienced military commander. He decided to carry out his father's plan, and his army headed for Persia in 334 BCE. Alexander's troops won every battle they fought, taking over all of Persia as

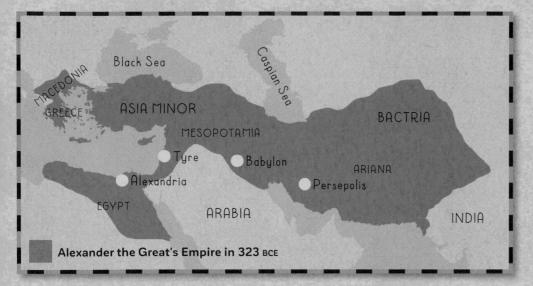

Alexander's conquered empire stretched from Greece in the west across Asia to India in the east.

SPREADING GREEK CULTURE

Alexander wasn't Greek, though some of his ancestors likely were. But as a teenager he was tutored by the Greek philosopher and scientist Aristotle, sparking a love of Greek culture. As he expanded his empire, he spread Greek literature, art, language, religion, and science over a large area. He set up dozens of new cities, many of which were named Alexandria in his honor.

Alexander tamed his horse Bucephalus as a boy, and he loved him so much that he named a city after him.

WHAT HAPPENED NEXT?

Alexander had not named an heir, and after his sudden death his generals split up the empire between them. Rebellions broke out in many places, and the huge empire that Alexander and his father had built soon crumbled. But his influence lived on in the way that many places continued to follow the Greek culture that he promoted. This was called the Hellenistic period (*Hellas* was the ancient Greek word for "Greece").

Ptolemy I ruled part of the empire after Alexander's death, including Egypt where he became pharaoh.

well as Egypt. It was a dazzling campaign, and his men were incredibly loyal, but by the time they reached India they'd had enough. The soldiers were homesick and refused to go any farther, so Alexander agreed to turn back. He died in Babylon in 323 BCE at the age of just 32.

ANCIENT ROME

Eventually controlling an area that stretched right across Europe, Western Asia, and North Africa, Rome formed one of the largest and most powerful empires the world has ever seen. But its beginnings were modest, coming in around 1000 BCE, when a group called the Latins arrived in the area around the Tiber River on the west coast of Italy. They founded a new city whose influence would expand hugely over the next millennium and a half.

The twins were said to have been abandoned as babies and raised by a female wolf.

ROMULUS AND REMUS

According to tradition, the city of Rome was founded in 753 BCE by a man named Romulus. He and his twin brother Remus were sons of Mars, the god of war. When they grew up, they wanted to build a city, but quarrelled about where it should be. Romulus killed Remus and built his own city, naming it after himself.

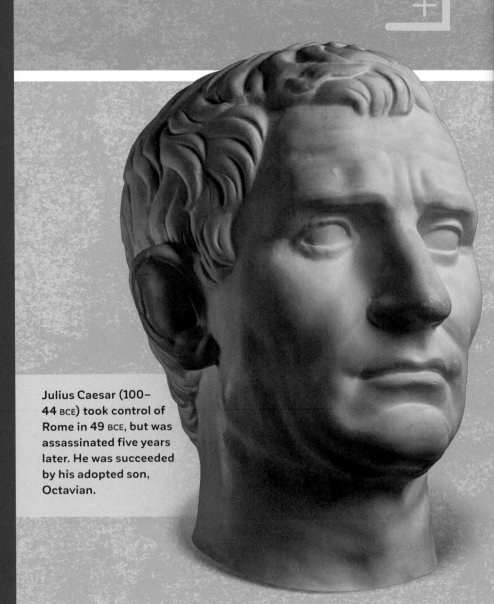

Julius Caesar (100–44 BCE) took control of Rome in 49 BCE, but was assassinated five years later. He was succeeded by his adopted son, Octavian.

FROM REPUBLIC TO EMPIRE

When Rome was just starting out, a more powerful group called the Etruscans lived to the north. The Romans copied many aspects of Etruscan culture and trade. At first, the city was ruled by kings, but in 509 BCE, the unpopular King Tarquin was overthrown and Rome became a republic—which means it was ruled by elected officials. This system lasted until 27 BCE, when a man named Octavian took over and renamed himself Augustus, turning Rome from a republic into an empire, with himself as sole ruler, the emperor. By this point, the Etruscans' land had been swallowed up and become part of Rome.

ROMAN LIFE

Romans were known for their building works, including roads and aqueducts, and their technology, including the use of steel. There were also poets, philosophers, and musicians. But Roman society had several different levels. The rich upper class had a good life, with beautiful homes and rich clothes. But the poorer people had it much harder. At the very bottom of the ladder were the slaves, who had no rights and were forced to work without pay.

Rich Romans liked to entertain and show off their homes, as shown in this French painting from 1783.

RELIGION AND BELIEFS

The Romans were experts at copying what they liked about other cultures—for example, Greek art—and adapting it to their own culture. They worshipped a large group of gods and spirits, a few of which were uniquely Roman. But many of the gods, such as Saturn, were taken from the Etruscans, and others, such as Hermes, were copied from the Greeks and renamed. The Romans believed that the gods controlled everyday life, and they offered sacrifices to keep them happy.

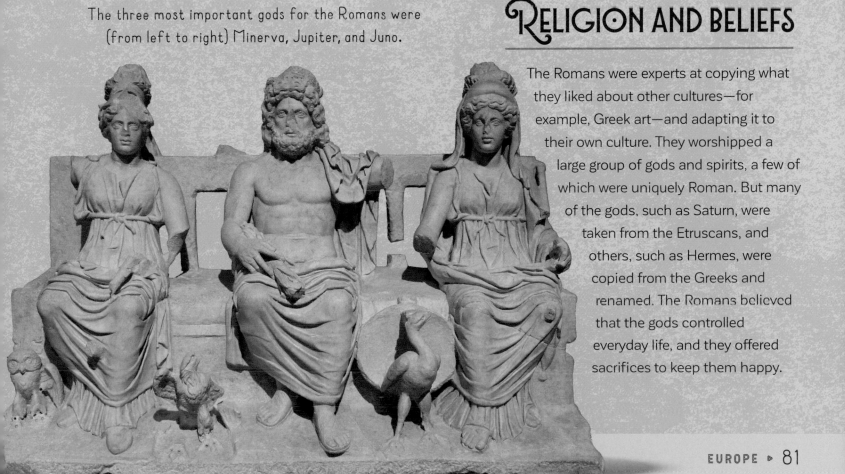

The three most important gods for the Romans were (from left to right) Minerva, Jupiter, and Juno.

The Roman Empire

Rome had started taking over new territories when it was still a republic. By the time Augustus became the first emperor (see pages 80–81), Rome controlled most of Spain, France, and Greece, as well as parts of Turkey, Egypt, and the coast of North Africa. The empire pushed these boundaries even farther in the next few centuries, taking over more territories, including Britain.

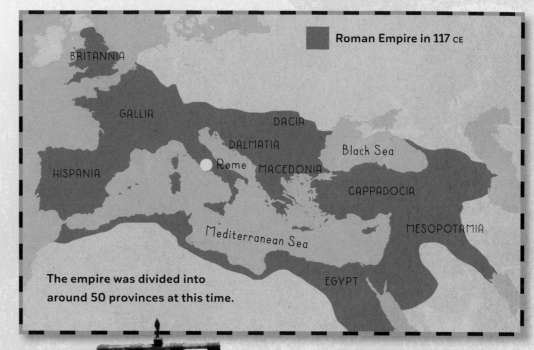

Roman Empire in 117 CE

BRITANNIA

GALLIA

HISPANIA

DACIA

DALMATIA

Rome

MACEDONIA

Black Sea

CAPPADOCIA

MESOPOTAMIA

Mediterranean Sea

EGYPT

The empire was divided into around 50 provinces at this time.

By 117 CE, the Roman Empire stretched from Britain (Britannia) in the north to Egypt in the south and from Spain (Hispania) in the west to Mesopotamia in the East.

The Roman Army

The Roman Empire was able to take over so much territory thanks to its large, powerful army. Unlike many other armies of the time, it was made up of full-time professional soldiers. Their rigorous training made them tough to beat. They wore armor and fought with swords and spears. They often fought in formations, such as a wedge for punching through enemy lines or the *testudo* (meaning "tortoise"). In this formation, soldiers stood in a tight group and used their shields to make a wall around and above them, like the shell of a tortoise.

This image a modern-day group of re-enactors dressed as Roman soldiers. The standard bearer at the front holds a flag with the name of the legion on it.

EMPERORS

The Roman Empire was ruled by a single emperor, and when he died the throne would pass to another. This was often a son or other relative, but sometimes generals or rivals would seize power instead. The emperor had immense power, but it was a dangerous job—more than half of them were either assassinated or died in battle. Some, such as Trajan and Marcus Aurelius, were widely respected as good rulers, while others, such as Caracalla (ruled 198–217 CE) were cruel and unstable.

Emperor Marcus Aurelius (ruled 161–180 CE)

PROVINCES

The Roman Empire grew so large that it could take months to travel from one end to the other. At first, the emperors ruled it by dividing it into provinces, each one ruled by a governor. This system worked for a time, but by 285 CE the empire was just too big for one person to handle. It split into Western and Eastern halves, each ruled by one of two co-emperors.

Gold coins such as these would be used to pay taxes that were sent back to Rome to fund the military and various building projects.

END OF EMPIRE

The Western Roman Empire was centered in Rome. In the late 300s, it began to grow weaker. Other groups began to invade—including the Visigoths, who sacked Rome in 410. The last emperor of the Western Roman Empire was overthrown in 476 CE. The Eastern Roman Empire survived for almost a thousand years as the Byzantine Empire, centered in Constantinople (now Istanbul). Its territory gradually shrank until it was eventually taken over by the Ottoman Empire, with Constantinople finally falling in 1453.

ROMAN ENGINEERING

Although the Roman Empire began more than 2,000 years ago, many of the structures they built are still standing. The Romans were master engineers who revolutionized the use of concrete —which they made using volcanic ash. They even made use of a type of concrete that could set underwater!

Parts of many Roman aqueducts are still standing, including the Pont du Gard, which was built around 40–60 CE in southern France.

ROADS AND AQUEDUCTS

The Romans built over 74,500 miles (120,000 km) of paved roads to connect the different parts of the empire. The roads were usually straight and were built up of layers of gravel covered in flat stone slabs. They often ran over and under bridges and through tunnels. The Romans also built aqueducts to carry water from mountains and springs into their towns and cities.

MILITARY ENGINEERS

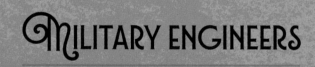

The Roman army benefited from the skills of its engineers. Every soldier carried a shovel as part of his basic equipment, and they were expected to build as well as fight. They constructed forts and fortified camps, and could build bridges quickly to help a military advance. Engineers designed and built machines for attacking fortified cities. Battering rams could knock walls down, while siege towers helped soldiers climb over them. Artillery weapons like the ballista could fling bolts or heavy stones over the walls.

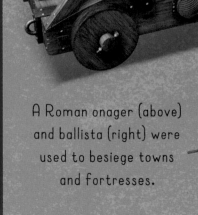

A Roman onager (above) and ballista (right) were used to besiege towns and fortresses.

URBAN LIFE

Many Romans lived in busy, crowded cities, full of many of the kinds of buildings that we still have today. Poor people often lived in apartment blocks called *insulae*, which could be more than five stories high. The bottom floors usually housed shops or fast-food restaurants called *thermopolia*. To keep clean, Romans went to public bathhouses with pools of different temperatures, heated by an underfloor system. There were temples for worship and theaters and arenas where they could watch plays, gladiator fights, chariot races, and other types of public entertainment.

Vitruvius

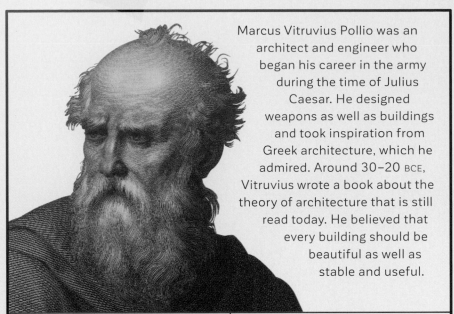

Marcus Vitruvius Pollio was an architect and engineer who began his career in the army during the time of Julius Caesar. He designed weapons as well as buildings and took inspiration from Greek architecture, which he admired. Around 30–20 BCE, Vitruvius wrote a book about the theory of architecture that is still read today. He believed that every building should be beautiful as well as stable and useful.

BORN:	DIED:
c. 80 BCE	c. 15 BCE

The ruins of the Colosseum, a giant arena for entertainments, still stand in Rome

CELTS

Celts were a collection of tribes who lived in central and western Europe during the Iron Age (see pages 14–15). These groups never formed a single kingdom or empire, but they were united by their language and culture. They had their origins in earlier cultures, such as the Urnfield culture (see page 67), but eventually spread westward throughout what is now France, Spain, and the British Isles.

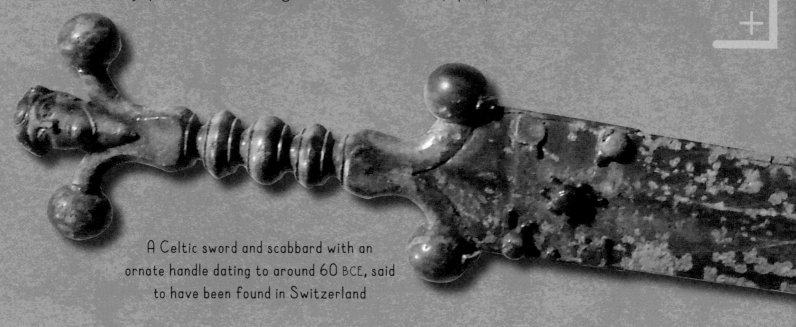

A Celtic sword and scabbard with an ornate handle dating to around 60 BCE, said to have been found in Switzerland

North Sea

Black Sea

Rome

Mediterranean Sea

■ **Area under Celtic control c. 275 BCE**

In the 3rd century BCE, Celtic tribes controlled most of Europe north of the Roman area.

TRIBES AND CHIEFS

These people didn't call themselves Celts—that was a name invented by Greek historians—but instead called themselves by the names of their individual tribes. Although tribes traded with each other and would sometimes band together to fight a common enemy, for the most part they stayed separate. Each tribe was ruled by a chief who would oversee farming and trade and lead them in battle. Some of these tribes eventually built large towns with defensive walls, and minted their own coins.

HERE COME THE ROMANS

The Celts were known as fierce warriors, often bleaching their hair and painting their bodies —and sometimes fighting naked!—to intimidate their enemies. They provided stiff opposition for Roman armies trying to take their land. But as the Roman Empire expanded, they conquered one Celtic group after another, folding them into the empire and overlaying their culture with Roman ideas. Only those living in Scotland and Ireland stayed independent, and versions of the Celtic language live on there today.

BOUDICA

Boudica was the wife of Prasutagus, king of the Celtic Iceni tribe, who lived in southeast England. When Prasutagus died in 60 CE, the Romans took over his kingdom. Boudica decided to fight back, and she raised a huge army to rebel against Roman rule. Her army burned London and several other Roman settlements before it was finally defeated at the Battle of Watling Street. Boudica died after the battle, probably by poisoning herself.

BORN:	DIED:
c. 30 CE	c. 61 CE

RELIGION

The Celts worshipped many gods, and they revered sacred natural places such as groves and springs. They also saw animals such as bulls, boars, stags, and horses as sacred. These animals were believed to have protective qualities and often appear on weapons and armor. When a person died, they were buried with items for the afterlife, including clothes, food, armor, and even board games. The Celtic religion was led by priests called druids who passed on their knowledge orally rather than by writing it down, so there is a lot we still don't know about it.

Important people were buried in mounds like this one at Hochdorf in modern-day Switzerland dating to around 530 BCE. The body was often laid in a four-wheeled chariot.

GERMANIC TRIBES

North of the Romans and east of the Celts lived many different tribes. Each had its own name, though the Romans referred to them all as *Germani*. They spoke closely related languages and shared many parts of their culture. But they never formed a unified empire.

MIGRATION AND EXPANSION

One thing that many of the Germanic tribes had in common was that, instead of building large cities, they lived in small farming communities. When their resources ran out, they moved on in search of new land to use for growing crops and raising animals. Migrating to new places like this often meant pushing out the people who already lived there. Germanic tribes were known as fierce warriors, using lances, swords, and round shields. Battle was important to them, and two of their most important gods —Odin and Thor—were gods of war and strength. After years of clashes with Rome, some of the tribes moved south as the Roman Empire crumbled in the fifth century CE.

A modern illustration showing the typical clothes and equipment of a Germanic warrior

Goths

The Visigoths were part of a larger group called the Goths. Roman writers divided them into two branches: the Ostrogoths in the east and the Visigoths in the west. In 410 CE, the Visigoths under their king, Alaric I, successfully invaded and looted the city of Rome. After sacking Rome, the Visigoths conquered large parts of France, Spain, and Portugal—taking some of them over from another Germanic tribe called the Vandals (see below). The Ostrogoths originally lived near the Black Sea, but they often invaded Roman territory. Under their leader, Theodoric, they took over most of Italy in 493 CE.

An ornate Visigoth gold crown from the seventh century CE

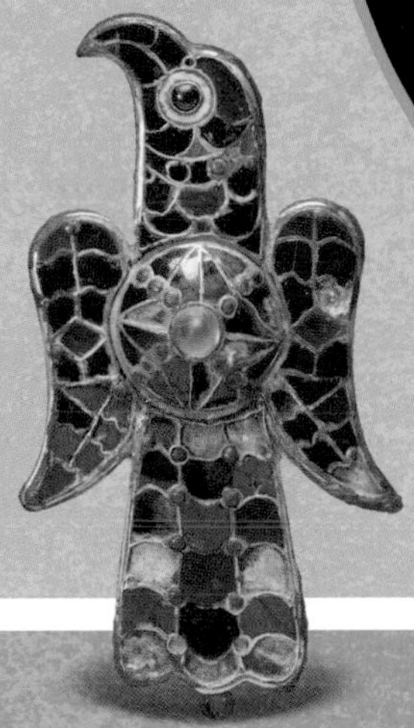

Found in an Ostrogoth grave in Spain, these sixth-century eagles were used to fasten a cloak.

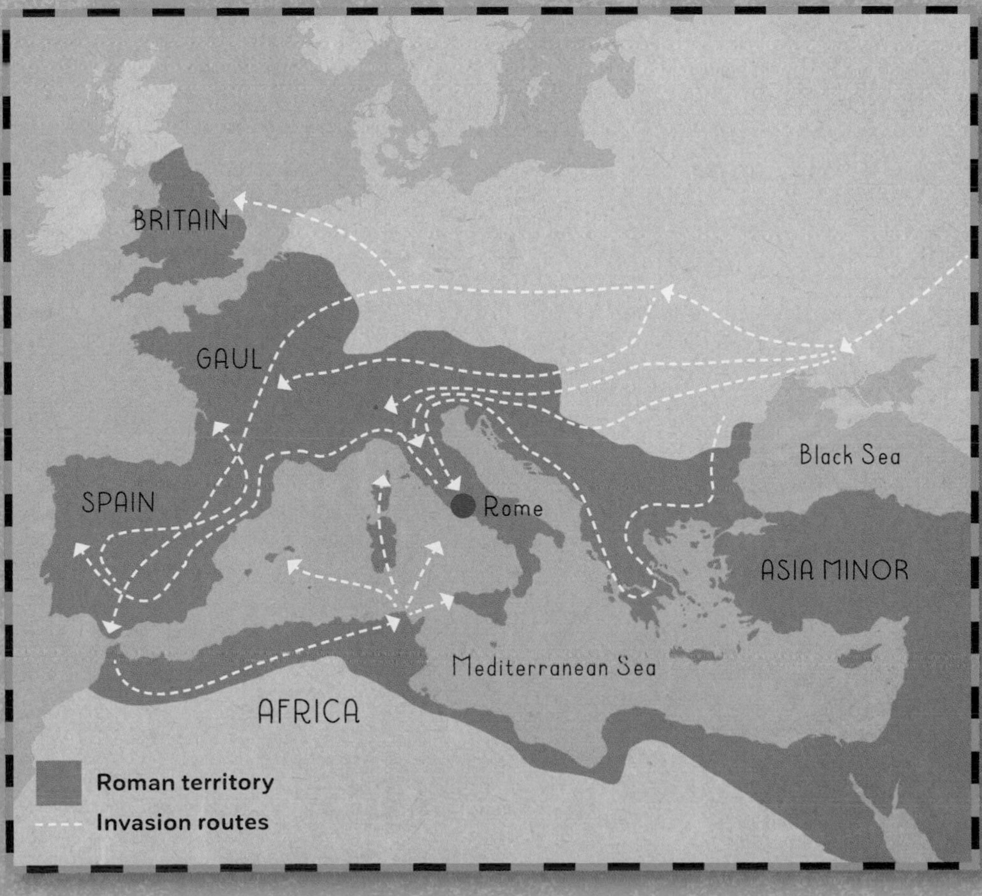

This map shows the invasion routes through Roman territory by various Germanic tribes during the fourth and fifth centuries CE.

Map labels: BRITAIN, GAUL, SPAIN, Rome, Black Sea, ASIA MINOR, Mediterranean Sea, AFRICA

■ Roman territory
--- Invasion routes

Vandals

The Germanic tribes did not use a written language, so most of what we know about their tribes, such as the Vandals, comes from Roman historians. They described the Vandals as violent barbarians (this is the source of our modern term "vandal") —not surprising when writing about an enemy. In 406 CE, after suffering from invasions by a group from central Asia called the Huns, the Vandals crossed the Rhine into the Roman Empire, hoping for safety. This set off a chain of clashes as they took over new land to settle, moving through France and Spain and into North Africa. In 455 CE, they entered Rome and looted the city.

VIKING ANCESTORS

The Viking raiders that terrorized northern Europe in the 9th and 10th centuries CE may have been the most famous culture to come out of Scandinavia, but they were by no means the first. Nearly 2,500 years earlier, nomadic people living here changed their lifestyle, settling down and setting up a wide trade network. This was the start of the Nordic Bronze Age.

A Scandinavian amber bead necklace dating from between the sixth and ninth centuries CE

The Amber Road

Amber is the fossilized resin from certain types of pine trees. It looks like drops of captured sunlight and is soft enough to be carved into beads and jewelry. Its rarity in most places made it valuable, and many people also thought it had magical or protective powers. Trade saw pieces of amber travel from the Baltic coast, near modern Lithuania, all the way south to Italy. From there it could go even farther —across the Mediterranean into Africa, or along the Silk Road to China. Amber from Scandinavia has been found in royal graves in Mycenae and Syria, and even in the tomb of Tutankhamun in Egypt.

RAW MATERIALS

It's not easy to start using bronze tools when you live in a land with no deposits of copper or tin. The technology for making and using bronze likely came from elsewhere —probably farther south. Once Nordic craftspeople learned to make bronze weapons and tools in around 1700 BCE, they needed a constant supply of raw materials, and this meant trading with other cultures. Their homeland may not have had much copper and tin, but it did have plenty of amber, and they traded it with other cultures.

SCANDINAVIA

Baltic Sea

Amber trade route

Venice

Adriatic Sea

Rome

Mediterranean Sea

Amber trade routes ran through Europe from c. 1500 BCE.

This bronze sculpture of a solar chariot was found in Denmark and dates to around 1400 BCE.

BRONZE AGE CULTURE

Historians aren't sure whether the Scandinavians carried their amber south, or whether traders from elsewhere visited to collect it. There are many petroglyphs (rock carvings) from this period that show ships, but it's impossible to tell how far people may have traveled in them. Most people during this time period lived in small farming communities made up of longhouses that could hold a family and their livestock. They supported themselves by farming, hunting, and fishing.

HONORING THE DEAD

People in Bronze Age Scandinavia sometimes buried their dead in large earthen barrows. Other bodies were placed in oak coffins and buried in wetlands, where the conditions preserved the bodies. They thought of bogs and wetlands as boundaries between this world and the next, making them ideal for burials and sacrifices, as the gods could easily collect any offerings. People were buried with items for the afterlife, including razors and combs, clothing, and even a bucket of beer.

Burial mounds like this one in Denmark (1370 BCE) were used for important people.

AFRICA

Africa is the birthplace of our species, the land where our earliest ancestors lived. Today it is home to more than 1.2 billion people, who make up many different cultures and speak well over 1,000 different languages.

This map identifies areas within civilizations featured in this chapter. Turn to the listed pages to see their full extent and to find out more about them.

Tutankhamun (see page 98)

ANCIENT EGYPT
pp94-99

Nubian statue (see page 101)

NUBIAN KINGDOMS
pp100-101

CARTHAGE
pp102-103

Malian horse and rider (see page 109)

MALI EMPIRE
pp108-109

GHANA EMPIRE
pp106-107

KINGDOM OF AXUM
pp104–105

Carved obelisks from Axum (see page 105)

GREAT ZIMBABWE
pp110–111

Carved eagle from Great Zimbabwe (see page 111)

DISTANT ANCESTORS

Paleontologists have found human fossils in Africa dating back tens of thousands of years, as well as much older fossils of the species we evolved from. But archaeologists in Africa also study more recent remains, of the cultures that developed there in ancient times. From Egypt in the north to Zimbabwe in the south, Africa is full of fascinating history.

ANCIENT EGYPT

Most of North Africa is a vast desert, but the land around the Nile River is rich and suitable for farming. It was on its banks that people began to set up farming communities around 5000 BCE. They would eventually grow and develop into one of history's greatest civilizations.

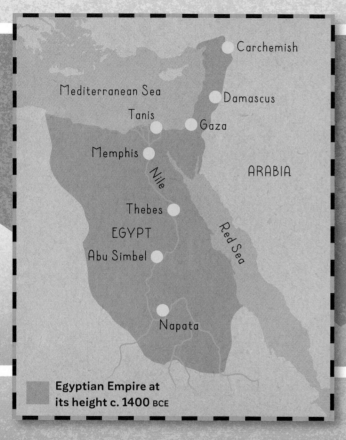

Carchemish

Mediterranean Sea

Damascus

Tanis

Gaza

Memphis

ARABIA

Nile

Thebes

EGYPT

Red Sea

Abu Simbel

Napata

Egyptian Empire at its height c. 1400 BCE

START OF A CULTURE

The farming communities along the Nile gradually evolved into small kingdoms, which sometimes conquered each other, and sometimes joined as allies. Eventually there were just two large kingdoms left—Lower Egypt in the north, near the Nile delta, and Upper Egypt in the south. In around 3150 BCE, a king of Upper Egypt named Menes (or sometimes Narmer) conquered Lower Egypt to unite the land into a single kingdom for the first time. This was the start of an era known as the Early Dynastic Period. During this time, Egyptian writing, religion, and art took shape.

THE OLD AND MIDDLE KINGDOMS

Sometime around 2575 BCE, rulers called pharaohs began to build elaborate stone pyramids and monuments such as the Great Sphinx (right). The pharaohs were seen as semi-divine and wielded immense power, able to mobilize thousands of workers for their building projects. This time is known as the Old Kingdom. It came to an end in about 2130 BCE, and, after a short period of instability, the Middle Kingdom period began in about 1938 BCE.

TIMELINE

Early Dynastic Period
(c.3150–2600 BCE)

Old Kingdom
(2575–2130 BCE)

First Intermediate Period
(2130–1938 BCE)

Middle Kingdom
(1938–1630 BCE)

Second Intermediate Period
(1630–1540 BCE)

3150 BCE

2500 BCE

2000 BCE

THE NEW KINGDOM

The Middle Kingdom came to an end after invasions by a group from Syria known as the Hyksos. They brought innovations such as bronze weapons and horse-drawn chariots. But the Egyptians wanted to rule themselves, and they forced the Hyksos out in around 1539 BCE. This led to the New Kingdom period, when rulers such as Ramses II (c. 1303–1213 BCE) helped Egypt reach the height of its power.

Ramses II had this temple built at Abu Simbel. It has four giant statues of him at the front.

Many of the giant monuments in the Old Kingdom period were designed to honor the gods or show the pharaoh's power.

HATSHEPSUT

Nearly all pharaohs were men, but Hatshepsut, who ruled from 1473–1458 BCE, was an exception. She took the throne after the death of her husband, Thutmose II. In paintings and carvings, she is often shown with a man's body and beard—a symbol of her power. Hatshepsut's reign was largely a time of peace in Egypt.

BORN:	DIED:
unknown	1458 BCE

New Kingdom
(1539–1075 BCE)

Third Intermediate Period
(1075–656 BCE)

Late Period, Ptolemaic (Greek) and Roman

1500 BCE   1000 BCE   500 BCE   1 CE

FARMING

Every summer, the river would flood, depositing layers of rich soil on the banks. When the waters receded, it was here that Egyptian farmers grew crops such as wheat, barley, beans, lentils, and fruits and vegetables. They dug channels to direct flood water to their fields and used a tool called a shaduf to move water from the canals onto the farmland.

LIFE ALONG THE NILE

The modern-day country of Egypt is mainly desert, and more than 90 percent of its population lives either in the narrow strip of land on either side of the Nile, or in the wide delta where the river meets the sea. In ancient times it was no different. The Egyptians depended on the river's water for drinking and washing. They also used it for transport, with boats carrying people and goods up and down the kingdom. Without the Nile, there would have been no Egyptian civilization.

Ancient Egyptian art often showed scenes from daily life including farming of the land.

PAPYRUS

One important crop was a reedlike plant called papyrus that grows in shallow water. The Egyptians wove its stalks into baskets, boats, rope, and mats. They also used the pith inside the stalks to make a writing surface that is also known as papyrus. In the days before paper was invented, this is what the Egyptians used—in fact, our word "paper" comes from "papyrus." Many examples have survived, allowing us to read about their history and culture.

Sheets of papyrus were used to record information using a picture-based writing system based on symbols called hieroglyphs.

GODS AND GODDESSES

The Egyptians believed in gods that controlled all aspects of daily life, including natural forces such as weather. The Nile was so important to them that they believed it was a gift from the gods, and there were several gods that controlled it. There was Khnum, the god of water, who created humans from wet clay; the crocodile-headed Sobek, who was linked with marshes and wetlands; and Hapi, who was the god of the annual flood.

Khnum   Sobek   Hapi

SACRED ANIMALS

The Egyptians considered many animals to be sacred, including cats, baboons, and ibises. Egyptian gods and goddesses are often shown with human bodies but the heads of various animals. For example, Anubis, the god of the dead, has the head of a jackal (see page 99) and Horus, the god of the sky, has a falcon's head, while Hathor, the goddess of love, has the head of a cow and Sekhmet a lion's head. This may have been a way of showing what these deities' powers and personalities were like.

Animals such as cats were sometimes mummified (see page 98) in the same way that human bodies were preserved.

Pyramids and Tombs

The ancient Egyptians believed that when a person died, their spirit or soul would live on in the afterlife. If they had lived a good life, they would go to a place called the Field of Reeds. But if they were judged by the gods to be unworthy, their heart would be eaten by a fierce monster. The Egyptians often built elaborate pyramids and tombs to honor and remember the dead and to give them the best chance in the afterlife. Archaeologists have found and excavated many of these tombs over the years. Most of the richest tombs were robbed of their treasures centuries ago, but others still contain mummies and the objects left to accompany the dead person into the afterlife. These finds tell us a lot about ancient Egyptian beliefs about death and the afterlife.

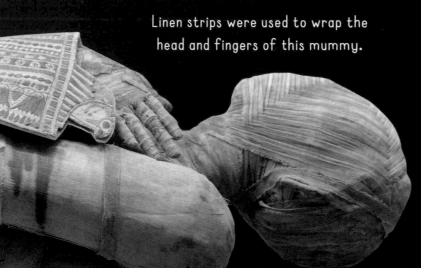

Linen strips were used to wrap the head and fingers of this mummy.

Mummies

Egyptians believed that if the dead body was prepared in the right way, the soul would return to it and the person would be reborn. Skilled workers would remove the internal organs and use salt to dry the body. Then it would be wrapped in linen strips to make a mummy. The mummy was placed in a coffin and then buried.

Rich and Poor

The bodies of the poor were buried in simple graves. But the richer you were, the grander your send-off. The mummies of rich and important people were laid in beautifully decorated coffins, or sometimes even a carved stone sarcophagus. They might have a brick tomb built over the burial pit. These tombs included a burial chamber and a chapel-like room where friends and relatives could leave offerings.

This golden mask was made for the pharaoh Tutankhamun (c. 1341–1323 BCE)

These pyramids were built as elaborate tombs for Egyptian pharaohs. Khufu's pyramid is on the right.

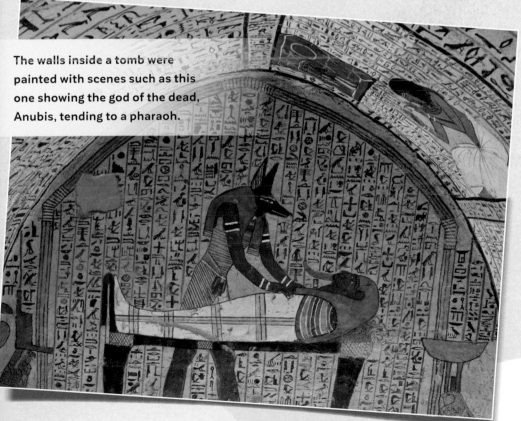

The walls inside a tomb were painted with scenes such as this one showing the god of the dead, Anubis, tending to a pharaoh.

Valley of the Kings

In the Old Kingdom, pharaohs built enormous pyramids. The burial chambers were hidden away deep inside, down narrow tunnels. The largest pyramid, built for the pharaoh Khufu, stood nearly 492 ft (150 m) tall. But in the New Kingdom, pharaohs began cutting tombs into the rock walls of a valley near Thebes. It became known as the Valley of the Kings. These tombs were elaborate on the inside, but the entrances were hidden, to keep tomb robbers away.

Supplies for the Afterlife

The Egyptians buried their dead with things they would need in the afterlife, such as food, clothing, makeup, and jewelry. Pharaohs were used to having servants, and in the early days their servants were killed and buried with them. Later, they used little figurines called *ushabtis* to represent the servants instead.

The doll-sized ushabtis could be made from wood, stone, or glazed ceramics.

NUBIAN KINGDOMS

Travel south along the Nile, past the Egyptian cities of Memphis, Thebes, and Luxor, and eventually you'll come to the region once known as Nubia. People also lived along the river's banks here, setting up farming communities around 5000 BCE—about the same time this was happening in Egypt. The history of Nubian kingdoms is intertwined with that of Egypt, but the Nubian people had their own culture and traditions.

KERMA

The remains of the walled city of Kerma.

Nubia is rich in gold, and its location near caravan trading routes made it a gateway for goods such as incense and ivory, which came from farther south. The Nubians were known for their archery skills, so the Egyptians called the region *Ta-Seti*, which means "land of the bow." The first advanced civilization in Nubia, the Kingdom of Kerma, developed in around 2500 BCE and had its center in the walled city of Kerma, home to up to 10,000 people. Its people worshipped Amun, the same sun god as in Egyptian culture. The kingdom came to an end in 1504 BCE, when the Egyptians destroyed Kerma and made the region part of their empire.

As in Egypt, the Nubians built pyramids as tombs for their rulers, but Nubian pyramids were smaller and had steeper sides.

Mediterranean Sea

EGYPT

Nile

Red Sea

Kerma
Napata

KUSH Meroe

■ **City of Kush c. 700 BCE**

■ **Kushite Empire's greatest extent c. 700 BCE**

MEROE

The last Kushite pharaoh, Tantamani, was defeated when the Assyrians (see pages 28–31) invaded Egypt in around 666 BCE. The Assyrians sacked the capital, Thebes, forcing Tantamani to flee south. This was the end of Nubian rule in Egypt and, in 593 BCE, the Egyptians invaded Nubia and sacked Napata. The Nubians set up a new capital at Meroe, farther south. This new kingdom had a culture that was less Egyptian and more Nubian, with its own written language.

A statue of the Nubian ruler Taharqa who ruled over Egypt from 690–664 BCE.

KUSH

Kerma was conquered when Egypt was entering its most powerful era, known as the New Kingdom period (see pages 94–95). But by around 1069 BCE, Egypt had grown much weaker because of drought, famine, and invasion. A new Nubian kingdom, Kush, arose with its capital in the city of Napata and, in 712 BCE, it conquered Egypt, meaning that Kushite kings were now pharaohs in Egypt. After so many years being ruled by Egypt, the Kushite culture was now very similar—they used the same writing system and worshipped many of the same gods.

Gold jewelry found on the mummy of Nubian King Amaninatakilebte (reigned 538–519 BCE).

CARTHAGE

The city of Carthage is on the north African coast, in modern-day Tunisia. According to legend, it was founded in 814 BCE by Dido, a queen of Phoenicia (see pages 34–35). She had fled her home in Tyre for the Tunisian coast, where the local chieftain told her that she could have as much land as an ox hide would cover. Dido cunningly cut the hide into thin strips and used them to encircle a large area, where she built a city for her people.

This painting from around 1720 shows Dido cutting up the ox hide into thin strips to mark out the area of her new territory.

BUILDING AN EMPIRE

Carthage was originally a minor port where Phoenician ships stopped for supplies or repairs. But its safe harbor and its location on important shipping routes helped it grow. By the time Alexander the Great (see pages 78–79) conquered Tyre in 332 BCE, Carthage was already powerful and it soon became the main power in the region, with colonies all along the Mediterranean coast.

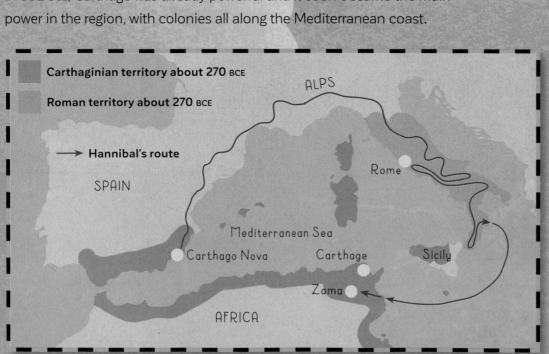

Carthaginian territory about 270 BCE

Roman territory about 270 BCE

→ Hannibal's route

ALPS

SPAIN

Rome

Mediterranean Sea

Carthago Nova

Carthage

Sicily

Zama

AFRICA

This maps shows the western Mediterranean during the Punic Wars. The conflicts with Rome are known as the Punic Wars, after the Latin name for the people of Carthage, which was *Poeni*.

Conflict with Rome

Rome was growing at the same time as Carthage, and it wanted to expand into Sicily. In 264 BCE, a series of wars between the two powers began. The Romans had little experience fighting at sea, but they were still able to defeat the powerful Carthaginian navy in 241 BCE and take over Sicily. Before long the Romans took over Carthage's colonies in Sardinia and Corsica, and another war began. This time it was mainly fought on land, in Italy and Spain, and it ended in another Roman victory in 202 BCE.

A 1773 American painting showing Carthage defeating Rome at the Battle of Cannae in the Second Punic War.

The Final Battle

Not long after its defeat, Carthage began to grow in strength again. The Romans were wary of the city regaining its former power, so they ordered that it be dismantled and rebuilt farther inland to disrupt trade. The Carthaginians refused and a third war began in 149 BCE. After three years of fighting, the Romans destroyed the city, ending the Carthaginian Empire.

Hannibal

In the second war with Rome, the Carthaginian army was led by the general Hannibal. In 218 BCE, he and a large army—which included dozens of elephants—set off from Spain. Instead of attacking Rome from the sea, they traveled overland, crossing the Alps. The march was successful, and Hannibal won several battles, but he and the Carthaginians were eventually defeated. After a lifetime of fighting the Romans, Hannibal committed suicide 183 BCE to avoid being captured.

BORN:	DIED:
247 BCE	183 BCE

Today, only ruins remain where the once mighty city of Carthage stood.

KINGDOM OF AXUM

Around 100 CE, a new power arose in the land that is now Ethiopia and Eritrea. This was the Kingdom of Axum (sometimes spelled Aksum). From humble beginnings, it grew until it included parts of what are now South Sudan, Sudan, Yemen, and Saudi Arabia. The kingdom —along with its strong navy—was known throughout the ancient world as a great trading power.

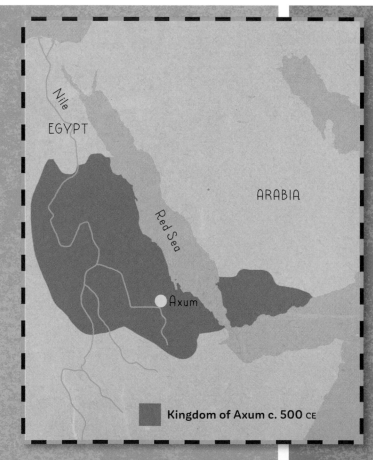

Kingdom of Axum c. 500 CE

At its height, the Kingdom of Axum covered most of modern-day Ethiopia and stretched up into Egypt and across the Red Sea.

LINKING EAST AND WEST

The capital city, also called Axum, was located on a high plateau. It sat at the crossroads of many different trade routes —by boat via the Red Sea and Nile river, as well as overland by caravan from the interior and southern parts of Africa. This meant that goods from all over Europe, Asia, and Africa passed through Axum. Its people exported gold, ivory, rhinoceros horns, emeralds, and salt. In turn, they imported iron, glass, wine, jewelry, textiles, and spices. The kingdom minted its own coins (see above), which have been found as far away as India.

Axumite craftworkers produced and exported simple red pottery.

These coins show King Ezana of Axum and were made in around 330–360 CE. They feature the Ge'ez script.

NEW IDEAS

The people in this region originally used a script called Sabaean, which came from southern Arabia, to write down their language. They sometimes used Greek as well. But at some point, early in the kingdom's history, the Axumites developed their own script, called Ge'ez. It is read from left to right and is still used in Ethiopia today.

ALL GOOD THINGS...

By the late 500s, the Kingdom of Axum was in decline. Historians aren't quite sure why, and it may have been a combination of different factors, such as poor harvests, invasions by peoples from the west, rebellions of conquered chiefs and competition with Arab peoples for trading routes. Whatever the causes, by the time the eighth century came to a close, the empire that the Axumites had built up was gone.

A NEW RELIGION

As the Kingdom of Axum was establishing itself, traders and missionaries brought a new faith called Christianity to the region. The Axumite people worshipped their own pantheon of gods, which included Mahram, Hawbas, and Astar. However, Christianity slowly grew in popularity, and in around 350 CE, King Ezana I converted to Christianity. His kingdom became the first civilization in sub-Saharan Africa to officially adopt Christianity.

Before adopting Christianity, the Axumites set up tall carved stone obelisks as markers for underground burial chambers.

WEST AFRICAN EMPIRES

A modern camel caravan, of the type once used in the Ghana Empire, shown trudging across the desert.

Empires rise and fall over time, and West Africa is no exception to this rule. Between 600 CE and 1600 CE, three great empires arose in this region. All became rich, thanks to one natural commodity: gold.

GHANA

The Ghana Empire was not located in the modern country of Ghana, but was farther northwest, in what are now the southern parts of Mauritania and Mali. Here, the regular flooding of the Niger River provided fertile land for farming. Over time, communities grew into kingdoms, and by the 800s an empire had been established. The capital was probably the walled city of Koumbi Saleh, which may have had a population of more than 50,000 people at its height. This was where the king lived, ruling over the surrounding villages, helped by a well-trained army.

This map shows trade routes across the Sahara in around 1100–1500 CE. These converged on the Ghana Empire, making it very rich and powerful.

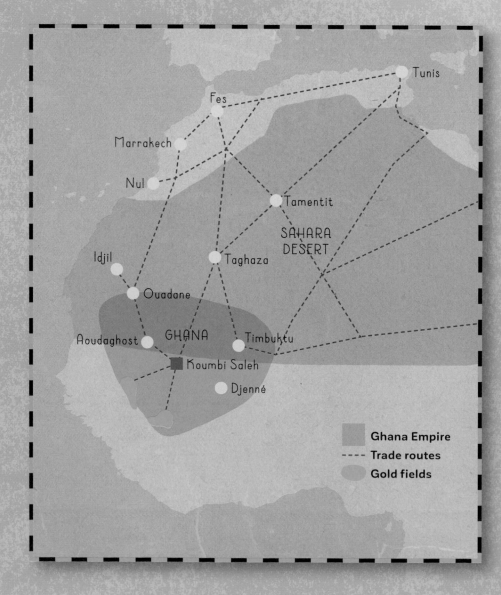

Tunis
Fes
Marrakech
Nul
Tamentit
SAHARA DESERT
Idjil
Taghaza
Ouadane
Aoudaghost
GHANA
Timbuktu
Koumbi Saleh
Djenné

Ghana Empire
- - - - Trade routes
Gold fields

LAND OF GOLD

The area to the south of the Ghana Empire had rich natural deposits of gold. Any large nuggets found in the mines belonged by law to the king, but merchants could trade gold dust—which is why people outside Ghana often knew it as the "Land of Gold." Using camel caravans, Ghanaian merchants set up trade networks across the Sahara to export gold as well as ivory, copper, iron tools, spices, nuts, and textiles.

CLASH OF CULTURES

By the 800s, the religion of Islam had been established in Arabia and had begun to spread elsewhere. Muslim merchants spread their religion as they traded with people throughout Africa. The kings of Ghana probably did not convert, but they must have tolerated the new religion because, after about 1050, remains at Koumbi Saleh show that the city was divided into a Muslim section, with many mosques, and another section where the kings lived.

The salt brought to Ghana may have been cut from mines in large slabs, like these ones.

THE SALT TRADE

Today, salt is such a common condiment that we take it for granted, but long ago it was a prized commodity. Salt was used to preserve food, but many places—particularly those far from the sea—had no easy supply. This meant that there were times when salt was literally worth its weight in gold. The caravans that carried gold north across the Sahara from Ghana brought salt back on their return.

Out with the Old, in with the New

The Ghana Empire (see pages 106–107) became less powerful in the 1100s. Years of drought affected its food supply, and it faced competition from new trade routes farther east. There were also civil wars, possibly caused by conflict between traditional beliefs in natural spirits and the new religion of Islam. The stage was set for a new power to take over and, in 1240, Sundiata Keita, a prince of the Malinke tribe, gained control of the old capital of Ghana and founded a new power that flourished from 1226–1670: the Mali Empire, as shown on this map.

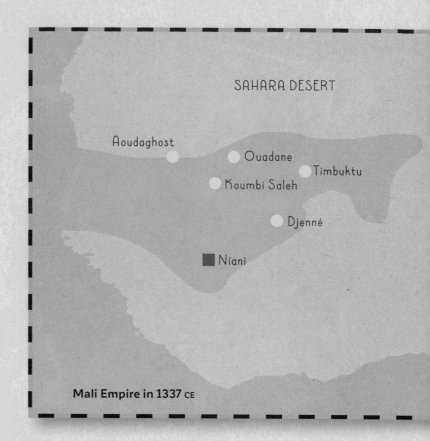

SAHARA DESERT

Aoudaghost

Ouadane

Timbuktu

Koumbi Saleh

Djenné

Niani

Mali Empire in 1337 CE

Starting Fresh

Sundiata Keita chose the city of Niani as his capital, and he set up a code of government, with rules for how people had to behave. Like the Ghana Empire, the new Mali Empire became powerful by controlling trade in gold and other materials—but it was more successful and, in time, became the largest and richest empire West Africa had seen. Its rulers forged strong links with the Islamic world with cities like Djenné and Timbuktu growing into centers of learning. By the 1300s, the Mali Empire became predominantly Islamic.

This mosque in Timbuktu is made of mudbrick and dates back to 1327 and the time of the Mali Empire.

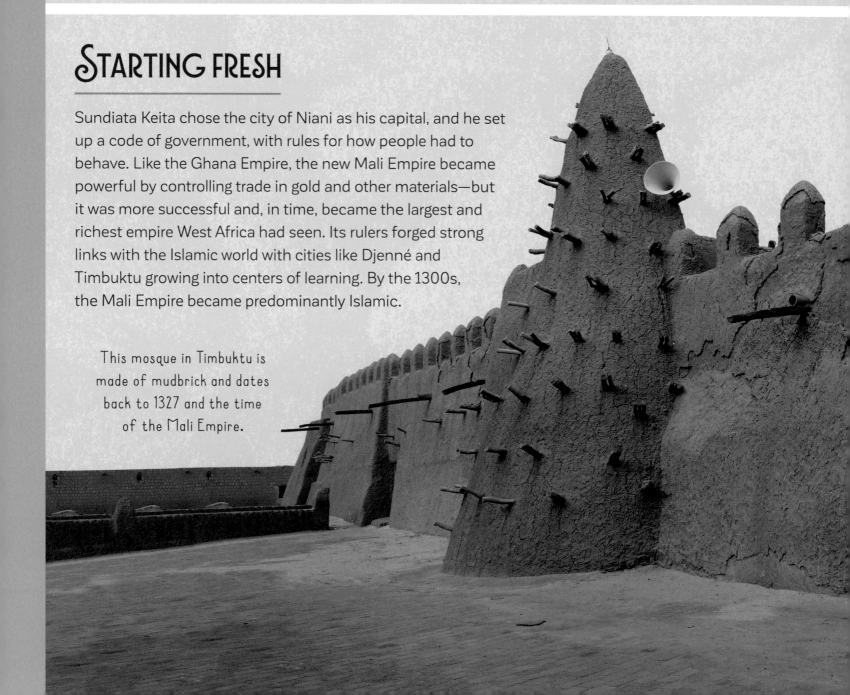

Mansa Musa

Mansa Musa I ruled Mali from 1312–1337, when the empire was at its richest ("mansa" is the word for "king" in the Maninka langauge of Mali). Helped by a strong army, he doubled the size of his territory. It's believed that he may have been one of the richest people in history. He spent so much gold during a pilgrimage to Mecca, Saudi Arabia, in 1324, that the value of raw gold crashed! After his pilgrimage, he brought back architects and Islamic scholars to build mosques and universities.

BORN:	DIED:
late 1200s	c. 1337

This horse and rider was made in Djenné during the Mali Empire.

Songhai

Mali's golden age couldn't last forever. In later years, there were often arguments over who the next ruler would be, leading to civil war. Mali's camel caravans were facing competition too —Portuguese trading ships now sailed down Africa's west coast, providing a more efficient way to get goods to the Mediterranean. The empire began to crumble, and in around 1468, King Sunni Ali of the neighboring Songhai Empire conquered what was left of it, including Timbuktu and Djenné. The Songhai Empire lasted until around 1591, when it was attacked and absorbed by the Moroccan Empire to the north.

GREAT ZIMBABWE

Many of history's best-known African cultures come from the north, where access to the Mediterranean Sea let them trade with other cultures in Europe and Asia. But there were large-scale civilizations in other parts of the continent too. One of the most impressive was the city of Great Zimbabwe, built in what is now the country of Zimbabwe by the Shona people sometime around 1100.

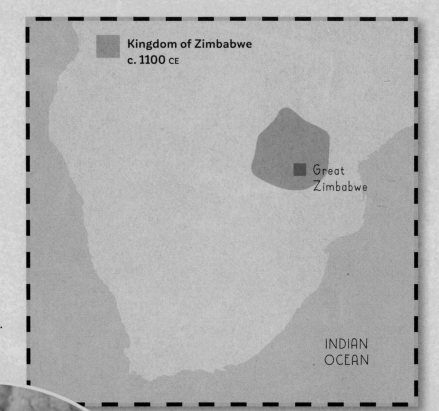

Kingdom of Zimbabwe
c. 1100 CE

Great
Zimbabwe

INDIAN
OCEAN

The disease caused by tsetse flies causes fevers, headaches, and joint pain, and can be fatal.

HEIGHT MATTERS

Dense jungle and poor soil made farming difficult in large parts of the continent south of the Sahara. This meant that relatively few large communities were able to emerge. Another problem was the tsetse fly, which spreads a disease called sleeping sickness through its bite. The disease affects both people and cattle. But the Shona people settled on a high plateau, about 3,300 ft (1,000 m) above sea level. That's too high for tsetse flies to live, so the Shona were able to raise cattle and crops.

CITY OF STONE

The settlement got its name from the Shona word *zimbabwe* which means "stone buildings." On a steep-sided hill, the Shona built a large complex from stone blocks, using no mortar. This is the oldest part of the site and was probably used for religious purposes. Farther down lies the Great Enclosure (below), a huge oval ring of thick, tall stone walls, with buildings inside. They include a 33-ft (10-m) tower (right)that is solid all the way through. Archaeologists are not sure what it was used for.

The walls of the Great Enclosure stretch for 820 ft (250 m) and are 32 ft (9.7 m) high in places.

END OF AN ERA

At some point during the 1400s, Great Zimbabwe was abandoned, but historians are not sure why. It may have been that the region's gold deposits ran out, or that the site was overpopulated or struck by drought. The Shona people moved a couple hundred miles to the north to set up a new kingdom, called Mutapa.

CONNECTED BY TRADE

The people of Great Zimbabwe traded the cattle they raised. They also exported local materials such as gold, elephant ivory, and animal skins with other cultures throughout Africa. In return, they received salt, seashells, pottery, glass beads, and other products. Once goods from Great Zimbabwe reached the east coast, they could travel even farther by ship—sometimes as far as China.

Several carved eagles have been recovered from Great Zimbabwe.

CROSSING OVER

Africa, Asia, and Europe are known as the Old World—where humans evolved and the first civilizations began. It took longer for our species to reach the "New World" of North and South America. For thousands of years, the New and Old Worlds existed without any knowledge of each other. The first humans to reach the Americas traveled from Siberia in Russia to what is now Alaska in the USA back when sea levels were lower than today and a "bridge" of dry land connected the two.

Carved in ivory bear (see page 131)

Mesa Verde (see page 128)

NATIVE AMERICAN CULTURES
pp130–131

ANCESTRAL PUEBLOANS
pp128–129

Aztec warrior (see page 123)

THE TOLTECS
p121

THE AZTECS
pp122–125

The Pyramid of the Sun, Teotihuacan (see page 120)

TEOTIHUACAN
p120

THE OLMECS
pp114–115

This map identifies areas within the civilizations and cultures featured in this chapter. Turn to the listed pages to see their full extent and to find out more about them.

Monks Mound (see page 127)

MOUND BUILDERS
pp126–127

THE MAYA
pp116–119

NORTH AMERICA

The people who came from Russia gradually spread throughout the continent of North America, developing into many different cultures. After sea levels rose and flooded the land bridge about 11,000 years ago, they were cut off from the Old World—at least until explorers in ships crossed the oceans to "discover" their complex cultures over 10,000 years later.

Maya jade mask
(see page 117)

THE OLMECS

The first civilization in the Americas grew along the Mexican coast. We still know relatively little about it—in fact, we don't even know what the people called themselves. It was the later Aztec people who called them Olmecs, a name that means "rubber people" because they harvested latex from trees to make natural rubber.

FARMERS

The Olmec civilization had its beginnings in around 2000 BCE, when people began farming maize on the banks of rivers. Before long, they were also growing beans and squash, and had started burning down sections of the rainforest to make fields. Agriculture meant that the Olmecs could produce surplus food, and this was stored in the settlements they built. It's likely that they had a system for organizing how it was shared out in times of need, possibly led by a chief.

An Olmec jade mask dating from around 800 BCE

CITIES AND TRADE

By about 1200 BCE, the Olmecs had built the city of San Lorenzo. It had workshops, homes, and a large building known as the Red Palace. In around 900 BCE, much of it was destroyed, and the city of La Venta became more powerful, controlling trade in the surrounding region. The Olmecs traded stone such as obsidian, jade, and mica, as well as pottery, rubber, and feathers. But by 300 BCE, La Venta had also been destroyed, and the Olmec civilization had faded away—though no one knows exactly why.

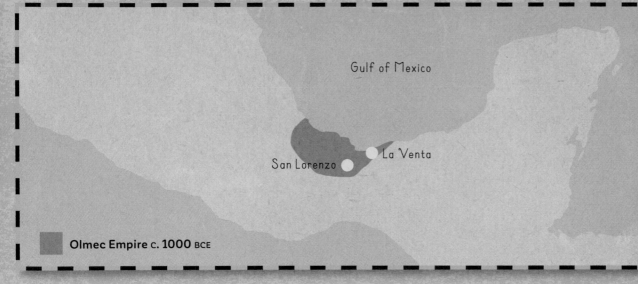

The Olmec people lived in an area of modern-day Mexico close to the shores of the Gulf of Mexico from around 1500–400 BCE.

Gulf of Mexico

San Lorenzo ● ○ La Venta

Olmec Empire c. 1000 BCE

☉LMEC ART

A lot of what we know about the Olmecs comes from the art they left behind. The most famous examples are the enormous stone heads, which may represent individual rulers. They are made from solid volcanic rock which had to be shaped without the help of metal tools. Smaller stone carvings and pottery figures often show people or powerful animals of the region, such as jaguars or eagles. Some of them show the were-jaguar, a mythical creature that is half man, half jaguar.

The biggest Olmec heads are more than 10 ft (3 m) tall and weigh several tons.

At La Venta, the Olmecs built a large pyramid that is one of the earliest known pyramids in the Americas.

ℙASSING IT ON

Even after the Olmec civilization faded away, it left a lasting impression. Many of its customs were carried on by later cultures who lived in the area. These include ceremonial ball games, blood-letting as part of religious rituals, making jade masks, and the layout of their pyramids and ceremonial buildings.

THE MAYA

At the same time as the Olmecs were building their civilization, another group was settling down in farming communities on the Yucatan peninsula to the east, which now covers areas of Mexico, Guatemala, and Belize. They were the Maya—a culture that flourished for many centuries and still lives on in the region.

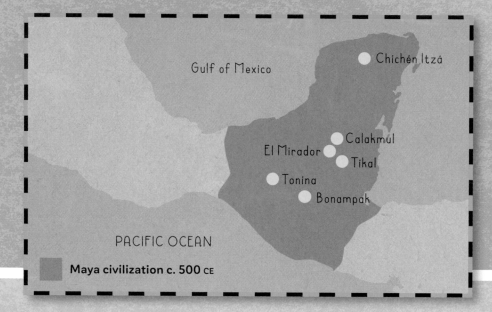

Gulf of Mexico

Chichén Itzá

Calakmúl

El Mirador

Tikal

Tonina

Bonampak

PACIFIC OCEAN

■ **Maya civilization c. 500** CE

Maya civilization was at its peak in around 250 CE and covered the Yucatan Peninsula of Mexico and stretched into modern-day Belize and Guatemala.

Some of the building work of the Maya was later covered by rainforest. Calakmul in Mexico was rediscovered in 1931 after being spotted from a plane.

FIRST CITIES

The first Maya farming villages date back to around 1800 BCE, and their settlements slowly spread through the region. They soon began building cities such as El Mirador in Guatemala, which dates back to at least 500 BCE, filled with temple–pyramids. The Maya "golden age," also known as the Classic Period, began in around 250 CE. During this period there were at least 40 cities, some home to 50,000 people. These were independent city-states, like the ones in Greece (see pages 72–77), but they shared the same basic culture.

TIKAL

The city of Tikal in Guatemala was built on land created by clearing an area of rainforest. Its location gave it access to natural resources such as cedar wood, incense, and flint, which its people could trade with other cities. Tikal was at its height from around 300–850 CE, conquering rival cities and setting up alliances. The city covered a huge area, with large plazas. There are temples, palaces, and ballcourts, as well as many smaller dwellings.

Like the Olmecs, the Maya made masks and other artifacts from jade.

JASAW CHAN K'AWIIL

The 26th *ajaw* (king) of Tikal was Jasaw Chan K'awiil, who ruled from 682–734 CE. He came to power at a time when Tikal was in decline, but he was a strong ruler who defeated the rival city of Calakmul in 695 CE, showing Tikal's continued strength. One of the large temples at Tikal served as his tomb, and another was the tomb of his wife.

BORN:	DIED:
before 682 CE	734 CE

CHICHÉN ITZÁ

After Tikal's power faded, the city of Chichén Itzá in Mexico became more powerful. In fact, by the 800s it may have been a kind of capital city, ruling over an alliance of neighboring city-states. At a time when few European cities had paved roads, the buildings in Chichén Itzá were connected by paved walkways. Many buildings are decorated with carvings of sacred animals, such as jaguars, eagles, and feathered serpents.

The pyramids built by the Maya, like this one at Chichén Itzá, were temples to their gods where rituals were performed.

Gods AND BELIEFS

The Maya worshipped a range of gods, who could change from human to animal shapes. These included Itzamna, the supreme creator; Kinich Ajaw, the Sun god; and Chac, the rain god. Worship sometimes involved human sacrifices. The Maya belief that life was a cycle, with nothing every truly dying, probably helped them to justify these practices. They believed that deep underground grew a "tree of life" that led to the heavenly paradise of Tamoanchan. To the Maya, anyone who died went on a journey toward Tamoanchan.

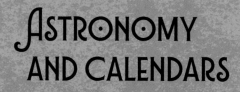

A statue of Chac, the Maya rain god from between 1200–1400 CE

Astronomy AND CALENDARS

Maya astronomers made careful observations of the Sun, Moon, stars, and planets, which they used to devise a complicated calendar system. The Maya had three different systems for marking time—a 260-day sacred calendar, a 365-day solar calendar, and another called the Long Count, which repeated every 5,128 years.

The Aztecs, who made this calendar disc, used a version of the Maya calendar.

Glyphs

Unlike many other American cultures, the Maya developed their own writing system, using symbols called glyphs. Some of the signs represent words or ideas, while others represent simple sounds. Most Maya scribes used about 500 different glyphs to record their history. They carved glyphs on stone, and they also wrote them on paper made from bark.

The Maya wrote on bark paper, which was folded into books called codexes. This rare example dates to between 900–1521 CE.

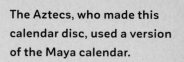

An open cacao pod
showing the beans

Chocolate

We have the Maya to thank for something very tasty! They were probably the first people to harvest the cacao bean and use it for making chocolate drinks. In fact, our word cocoa comes from the Maya word *KaKaWa*. However, their version of chocolate was different from ours. They didn't have sugar or milk, so they sweetened it with honey and added spices such as chilli.

Ball courts have been found at many Maya sites.

The Ball Game

Like other early cultures in Central America, the Maya played a ball game that is often called *pok-ta-pok* or *pitz*. It was played on a stone court, and two teams competed to score points by getting a rubber ball through a small ring placed high on the wall (right). Players were only allowed to hit the ball with their hips, elbows or knees. The game could be played for fun, but it also had religious meaning.

TEOTIHUACAN

While the Maya were building cities in the east, another culture was developing in what is now central Mexico. Teotihuacan began as a small settlement, sometime after 150 BCE. A natural spring provided plenty of water for drinking and irrigating crops. By 200 CE, it had grown to include large structures, such as pyramid-temples, laid out in a grid pattern. We known this city as Teotihuacan, although that is the Aztec name for it, meaning "place of the gods." We don't know what the people who lived there called it.

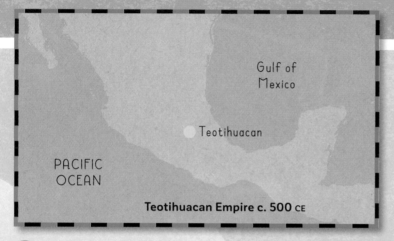

Gulf of Mexico

Teotihuacan

PACIFIC OCEAN

Teotihuacan Empire c. 500 CE

DOMINATING THE AREA

By about 500 CE, Teotihuacan was home to as many as 200,000 people, making it one of the world's largest cities. It became powerful through both trade and conquest. The city was located near a source of obsidian, a type of valuable volcanic glass used to make spear and dart heads. The soldiers in Teotihuacan's army, who wore distinctive feathered headdresses, launched these spears at their enemies using spear-throwers called atlatls. The people of Teotihuacan also traded the obsidian with other regional groups, along with cotton, cacao, feathers, salt, and crops.

This carving from Teotihuacan represents the feathered serpent god known as Quetzalcoatl.

The Pyramid of the Sun, built in around 200 CE, was the largest building in Teotihuacan.

END OF AN ERA

In around 600 CE, Teotihuacan's main buildings and sculptures were smashed and burned. This may have been an invasion by another group, or an uprising from within with city. People continued to live there, but it was no longer a regional power, and it was later taken over by the Aztecs.

THE TOLTECS

After the decline of Teotihuacan, a group called the Toltecs migrated to the area from the deserts to the northwest. The Toltecs sacked what was left of Teotihuacan in around 900 CE, and they built their own capital at Tollan—often called Tula. Although it was never as big as Teotihuacan, the city was laid out in a grid and looked similar to Chichén Itzá—a sign that there were cultural links between the Maya and the Toltecs.

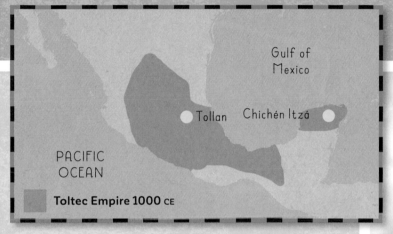

Gulf of Mexico

● Tollan   Chichén Itzá ●

PACIFIC OCEAN

Toltec Empire 1000 CE

City of Gold?

A few hundred years later, the Aztecs would tell stories about Tollan, saying that its buildings were made of gold, jade, and quetzal feathers. This is not true, but the Toltecs were skilled craftworkers and carved animals and human figures into the stones of their buildings. The Toltec Empire didn't last long, falling in 1168 CE, but the remains of its city show us what the culture was like.

Stone columns from Tollan show warriors dressed for battle, holding atlatls (spear throwers).

Toltec carvings of reclining figures are called chacmools.

THE AZTECS

After the end of the Toltecs, the next great empire in Mesoamerica (modern Mexico and Central America) was the Aztecs (also known as Mexica). They built a reputation as fierce warriors, controlling a large area of Mexico before their empire was destroyed by invaders from Europe.

The image of the eagle on the cactus appears on the modern flag of Mexico.

THE SNAKE AND THE EAGLE

Aztec legends say that they were originally hunter-gatherers from northern Mexico. After settling for a while near the ruins of Tollan, the Aztecs were told by their god Huitzilopochtli that they must leave and look for a new home. When they saw an eagle perched on a cactus with a snake in its beak, that was where they should build their city. And in 1325 they spotted exactly that, on an island in Lake Texcoco.

CITY ON A LAKE

The ruins of the ancient city of Tenochtitlán are found in the center of modern-day Mexico City.

The Aztecs built a temple on the site, followed by other buildings. They enlarged the available space for building by making artificial islands. They fenced off an area of lake, then filled it with layers of mud and other materials. They could grow crops or build on these "floating islands." Tenochtitlán grew and grew, in a grid pattern similar to other cities in the area. The buildings were connected to the lakeshore by raised roads called causeways. There were canals and an aqueduct that carried freshwater to the city from a nearby spring.

Gulf of Mexico

Tenochtitlán

PACIFIC OCEAN

Aztec Empire in around 1519

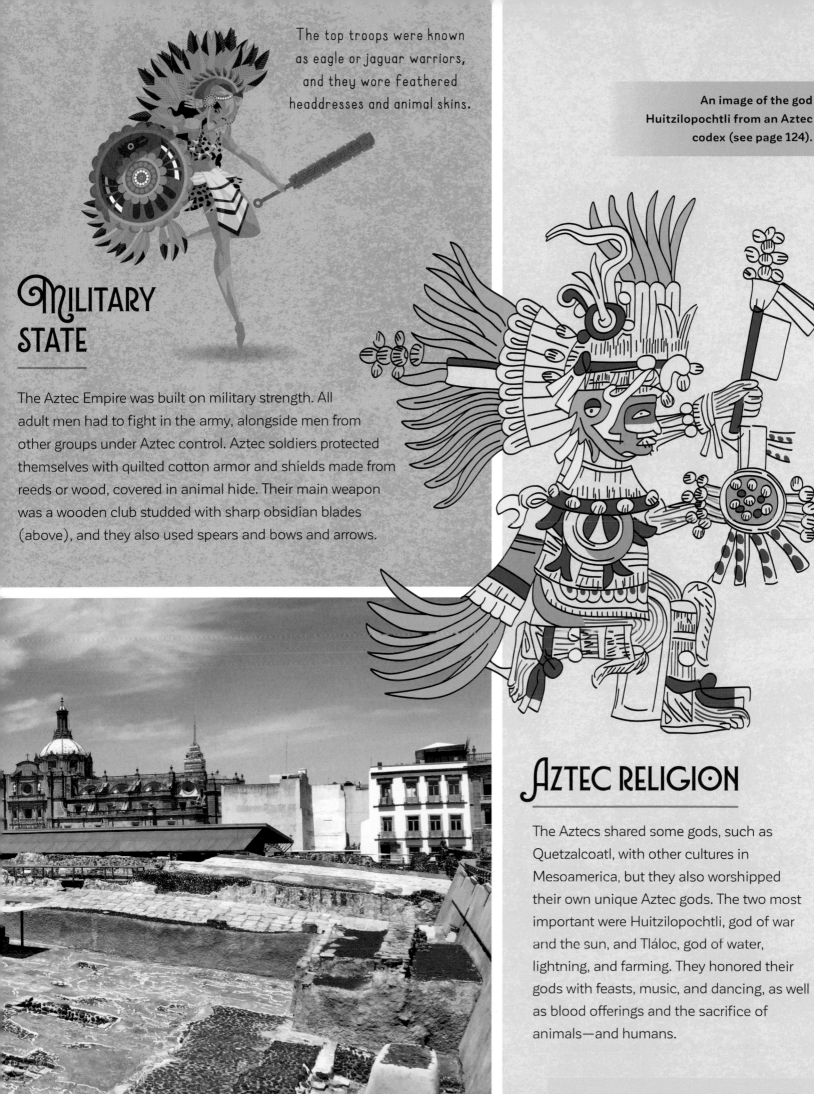

The top troops were known as eagle or jaguar warriors, and they wore feathered headdresses and animal skins.

An image of the god Huitzilopochtli from an Aztec codex (see page 124).

MILITARY STATE

The Aztec Empire was built on military strength. All adult men had to fight in the army, alongside men from other groups under Aztec control. Aztec soldiers protected themselves with quilted cotton armor and shields made from reeds or wood, covered in animal hide. Their main weapon was a wooden club studded with sharp obsidian blades (above), and they also used spears and bows and arrows.

AZTEC RELIGION

The Aztecs shared some gods, such as Quetzalcoatl, with other cultures in Mesoamerica, but they also worshipped their own unique Aztec gods. The two most important were Huitzilopochtli, god of war and the sun, and Tláloc, god of water, lightning, and farming. They honored their gods with feasts, music, and dancing, as well as blood offerings and the sacrifice of animals—and humans.

Europeans Arrive

In 1519, the Aztecs were at the height of their power when everything changed. European explorers had "discovered" the Americas 27 years earlier, and now a group of Spanish soldiers and explorers led by Hernán Cortés arrived in Tenochtitlán. At first, they were welcomed by the Aztec emperor, and they were impressed by the palaces, temples, and gardens of Tenochtitlán, describing it as the greatest city they had ever seen. However, the Spanish were not tourists—they were there to claim land and find gold for their king, and relations soon turned sour.

Art and Writing

Like other cultures in the region, the Aztecs carved large stone figures of people, animals, and gods. They were also known for their metalwork, in gold and silver. They believed that gold came from the gods and was connected to the power of the Sun. The Aztecs also had their own system of writing, based on pictograms—pictures that represent a word or idea. They produced bark-paper codexes (books), but most of these were destroyed by the Spanish. However, many people in Mexico still speak languages closely related to Nahuatl, the Aztec language.

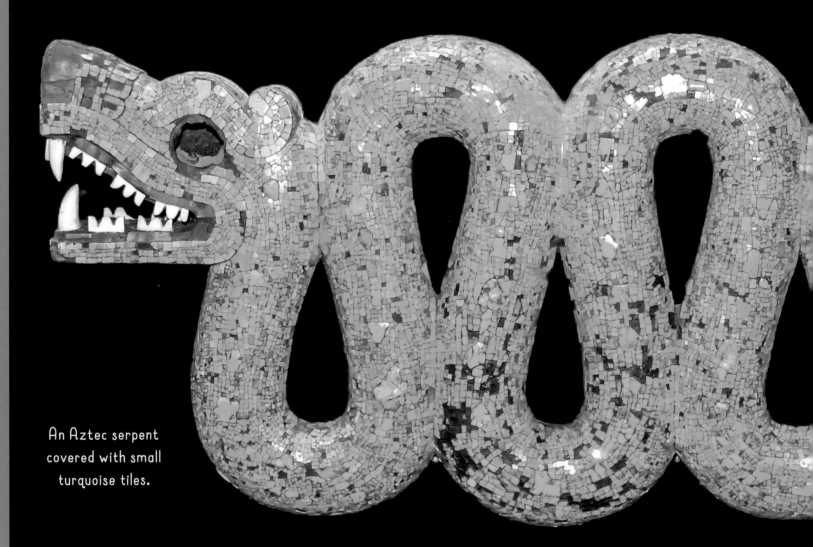

An Aztec serpent covered with small turquoise tiles.

Moctezuma II

When Cortés arrived, the Aztec emperor Moctezuma II had been on the throne for 17 years. He was commander of the army as well as head of the empire. Some of the tribes ruled by the Aztecs were unhappy with Moctezuma, and they formed alliances with Cortés. The Spanish held Moctezuma under a kind of house arrest, and he was killed in 1520—possibly by his own subjects, who were angry that he seemed to have given in to the Spanish.

BORN:	DIED:
c. 1466	1520

The End of the Aztecs

Cortés had only about 500 men, while Tenochtitlán was a huge city at the heart of a powerful empire. However, the Spanish had better weapons, including guns, crossbows, and steel swords and armor. They also rode horses, which the Aztecs did not. The Aztec forces were weakened by an epidemic of smallpox, a deadly disease brought by European explorers to which they had no natural immunity. After two years of fighting, with the help of other tribes who hated the Aztecs, the Spanish took control of Tenochtitlán in 1521. This was the end of the Aztec empire.

Rare examples of surviving Aztec artifacts include this gold serpent (left) and stone mask (below).

MOUND BUILDERS

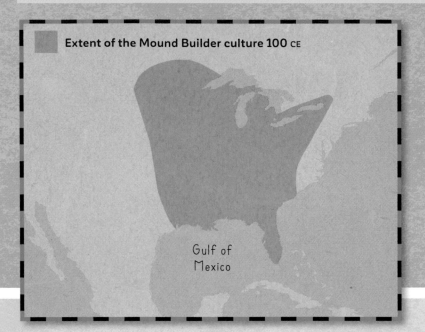

Extent of the Mound Builder culture 100 CE

Gulf of Mexico

At the same time that civilizations were emerging in Mesoamerica, farther north in the land that is now the eastern United States, people had begun building mounds out of earth. Some were fairly small, while the largest had a base bigger than the Great Pyramid of Giza. This practice started in around 3500 BCE and was shared by several different cultures over thousands of years.

Hunter Gatherers

The first groups to construct these mounds were not building cities. They were hunter-gatherers, moving around to find food. Many of the mounds were cone-shaped and served as burial sites for the dead. Over time, people started building bigger mounds. Some were built in the shape of animals, such as snakes or birds. These likely had a ceremonial purpose. In Louisiana, a group of hunter-gatherers built a collection of mounds that included ridges where homes were built.

This serpent-shaped mound in Ohio stretches more than 1,300 ft (400 m).

THE MISSISSIPPIANS

By about 700 CE, people in the Mississippi River valley were farming maize and settling down in towns and villages. These people, known as the Mississippians, also built mounds—some topped with wooden temples. Each settlement was ruled by a chief who also served as a priest. The Mississippians were spread out over a large area, and they were not an empire ruled by a single king. Instead, they were many independent groups who shared culture and beliefs, and who sometimes made alliances and sometimes fought with each other.

Examples of Mississippian pottery 800–1600 CE

The Mississippians had no wheeled vehicles or animals to pull them, so all the earth to build Monks Mound at Cahokia was carried by hand.

CAHOKIA

The largest Mississippian mound was at Cahokia (above), a site not far from the modern city of St. Louis. By around 950 CE, this prehistoric city was growing rapidly, and at its height about 20,000 people lived there. There are about 120 mounds in Cahokia, and the largest stands at the edge of a large rectangular plaza and is more than 100 ft (30 m) tall. At the top was a large wooden building—likely a palace for the ruler. Artifacts found at Cahokia show that they traded with groups that lived hundreds of miles away.

CULTURE AND BELIEFS

Historians think that most Mississippian groups shared a religion, likely spread through trading contacts. Artifacts with the same symbols turn up at a wide range of sites, including a winged "birdman" that might represent a god. Other symbols include a hand with an eye in the palm, a forked eye, and a circle with a cross in it.

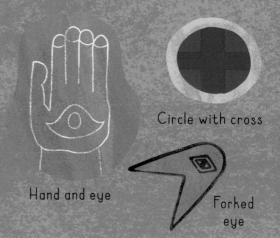

Circle with cross

Hand and eye

Forked eye

ANCESTRAL PUEBLOANS

In what is now the southwestern United States, another group was also building large structures at the time as the Mississippians farther east (see pages 126–127). But instead of piling earth into mounds, they used stone to build large, complicated dwellings. These are called pueblos (Spanish for "village"), and that is why historians call these people the Ancestral Puebloans.

Mesa Verde
Chaco Canyon

PACIFIC OCEAN

Ancestral Pueblo territory c. 1350 CE

Pueblo Bonita in Chaco Canyon was constructed from local sandstone.

Mesa Verde

A group known as the Basketmaker Culture first lived in the area. They began as hunter-gatherers but eventually settled in communities to grow crops, mainly maize, beans, and squash. By about 750 CE, they had started to build pueblos. These structures consisted of many adjoining rooms, sometimes more than one story tall. Some were built into the sides of steep-sided hills with flat tops known as mesas. At Mesa Verde (right) in what is now Colorado, the Puebloans built their homes in sheltered alcoves in the mesa's sides and grew crops on the mesa's top.

At Mesa Verde, people may have moved from the mesa top to the houses built in the cliff alcoves for defense, or for protection from the elements.

Puebloan sites have objects from far away, such as shell beads from California.

CHACO CANYON

About 100 miles (160km) to the southeast of Mesa Verde, another group of Ancestral Puebloans built homes at Chaco Canyon. The largest structure, called Pueblo Bonito, was mainly built in the 900s CE. It had about 800 rooms and would have housed hundreds of families. It shows clear signs of being planned in advance, rather than starting small and being added to gradually. Pueblo Bonito and the other structures in the area were connected by roads and were aligned with the points of the compass as well as with the positions of the Sun and Moon.

BELIEFS

Both Mesa Verde and Chaco Canyon have many round, semi-underground rooms called kivas. These were used for religious ceremonies, and people would enter through a ladder. They honored spirits called katsinas who represented ancestors or things in the natural world. They acted as a link between humans and gods.

END OF THE PUEBLOS?

Mesa Verde, Chaco Canyon, and other Ancestral Puebloan sites thrived for many years. But Chaco Canyon was abandoned in around 1150, and Mesa Verde in the late 1200s—probably due to a long period of drought in both cases. However, the Ancestral Puebloans continued their culture in other locations. Their descendants still live in pueblos today.

NATIVE AMERICAN CULTURES

By 1500, North America was home to several million people, who were split into hundreds of different groups and spoke many different languages. Each group had a way of life that was suited to the natural environment where they lived.

American cultural areas c. 1500 CE

IROQUOIS AND ALGONQUIN

Two large groups lived Northeast of what now makes up parts of Canada and the USA: the Iroquois and the Algonquins. Each was composed of many smaller groups that spoke closely related languages. Although Iroquois and Algonquin groups often came into conflict, they had similar lifestyles—hunting, fishing, gathering wild foods, and growing crops. None of their groups built cities, but Iroquois tribes lived in large longhouses built of wood and bark. Algonquin tribes set up smaller homes called wigwams or wickiups.

PLAINS NOMADS

On the vast plains in the center of the continent, some groups farmed and also hunted the bison that lived there. Once horses were introduced, brought by the Europeans, hunting bison became easier. Horses could also help drag sledges called travois, carrying a group's possessions from one camp to the next. Groups such as the Cheyenne became nomadic, following the bison herds. They ate the animals' meat and used the hides to make clothing and tents called tepees. They traded bison products for maize and other crops.

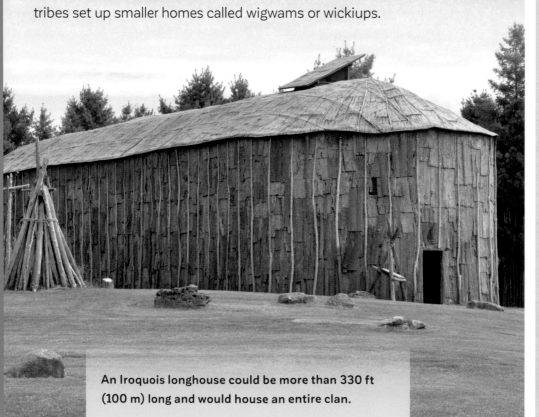

An Iroquois longhouse could be more than 330 ft (100 m) long and would house an entire clan.

Arctic Survivors

In the far north, the land is covered in snow and ice for large parts of the year. There are few trees or edible plants, but peoples such as the Inuit were able to survive here. Using skin-covered kayaks or larger boats, they hunted sea mammals such as seals, walruses, and whales. They also used bows and arrows to hunt caribou, which provided fur for warm clothing (left). They sheltered in animal-skin tents, and sometimes in semi-underground stone or earth houses, or even in domes made from blocks of snow during hunting trips.

A swimming bear carved in ivory by people in the Arctic, c. 1000 CE

European Encounters

This propagandist painting shows the Spanish explorer Hernando De Soto (on the white horse) becoming the first European to see the Mississippi River in May 1541, while anxious Native Americans look on.

When European explorers arrived in North America around 1500, they saw it as a land of riches. The native peoples were often seen as an obstacle. They suffered greatly from the Europeans, who brought guns as well as deadly diseases and would end up taking most of their land. However, a vibrant mix of Native American cultures still survives today.

SOUTH AMERICA

South America was the last continent to be reached by humans—apart from Antarctica, which was never permanently settled. Archaeologists still aren't sure when humans arrived here, but it was likely at least 14,000 years ago. In the time since then, a wide range of cultures and civilizations has spread across the continent.

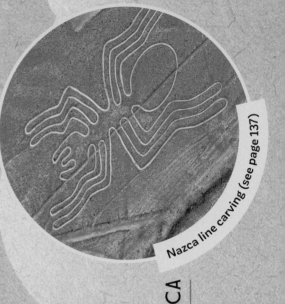

Nazca line carving (see page 137)

Paracas mummy (see page 135)

Moche pottery head (see page 136)

The Nazca
p137

Early Peruvian Cultures
pp134–135

The Moche
p136

THE INCA EMPIRE
pp138–141

Ceremonial Inca knife handle (see page 141)

This map identifies areas within the civilizations and cultures featured in this chapter. Turn to the listed pages to see their full extent and to find out more about them.

A VARIED LANDSCAPE

South America has a chain of high mountains known as the Andes running down its west coast, while much of the central and eastern part is covered in dense rainforest and there are vast grassy plains to the south. The continent is famous for its diversity of plant and animal life, but the human cultures that have called it home are equally diverse.

EARLY PERUVIAN CULTURES

West of the Andes in what is now Peru, a long strip of desert separates the mountains from the coast. It was here that some of the earliest permanent settlements in South America have been found. Unlike many other early settled cultures, these people depended more on fishing than they did on farming—a consequence of the landscape where they lived.

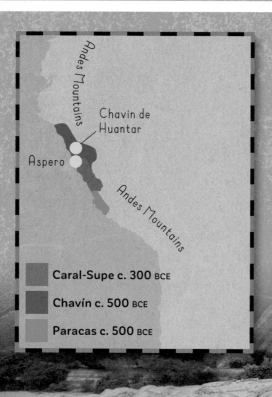

Andes Mountains

Chavin de Huantar

Aspero

Andes Mountains

■ Caral-Supe c. 300 BCE

■ Chavín c. 500 BCE

■ Paracas c. 500 BCE

CARAL-SUPE

One early group, known as the Caral-Supe, built at least 30 settlements along the coast. These settlements began in about 3500 BCE and became larger and more complex after about 3100 BCE. One site, known as Aspero, flourished between about 3000–2500 BCE. Like other Caral-Supe cultures, these people did not make pottery, but grew cotton plants, using the fibres to fashion clothing and fishing nets. They also made buildings out of stone. Some of the rooms in these buildings were decorated with colored paint and carvings.

The ruins of the sacred city of Aspero include large earthen platform mounds and sunken circular courts, as well as pyramid-like structures and homes for the wealthy and elite.

A Paracas mummy dating back to c. 400–100 BCE

Paracas

From about 900 BCE to 400 CE, the Paracas people lived on a thin strip of land that jutted out into the Pacific Ocean. Here, they developed systems for irrigating their crops and wove beautiful textiles. They used locally grown cotton as well as wool from llamas and alpacas which must have come from other cultures living high in the Andes. The Paracas people dyed their threads in brilliant colors and wove them on looms, using embroidery (stitchwork) to create pictures and patterns. Some of these textiles were used to wrap the mummies that the Paracas people buried with precious objects in tombs.

Chavin

Another group, called the Chavín, lived in the area from about 900–200 BCE. Their main city, Chavín de Huántar, is located in the highlands about 60 miles (100 km) from the coast at the place where two rivers meet. It was an important religious site for the surrounding area. One of its temples dates back to about 750 BCE and has several connected buildings forming a U-shape, with a sunken court in the middle. Carvings in the stone show creatures that have a mix of human and jaguar features. Inside the temple stands a 14.8-ft (4.5-m) obelisk (right) covered in images of mystical creatures. It probably held a religious significance, and people may have left offerings such as gold and shells at its base.

This obelisk was originally located in the courtyard of the Old Temple at Chavín de Huántar.

THE MOCHE

The next powerful group to appear, a bit farther north along the coast, was the Moche. This culture emerged in about 1 CE and flourished until around 800. Their capital city—also called Moche—lies at the foot of the Cerro Blanco mountain. Alongside houses, workshops, and storage buildings, there are two enormous pyramid-like mounds made of mud bricks. Each of the millions of bricks in these pyramids is stamped with a mark showing who made it. Both pyramids were built in around 450 CE and painted red, white, yellow, and black. At the top, religious rituals including human sacrifice were performed.

Andes Mountains

Moche

Andes Mountains

Moche culture
c. 500 CE

The Pyramid of the Sun is the taller of the two pyramids at Moche, standing more than 165 ft (50 m) high.

The Moche used molds to create pottery with detailed shapes such as human faces.

MOCHE ART

The Moche are known for their beautiful arts and crafts—everything from ceramics and textiles to tattoos and intricate metalwork. Some pottery vessels were painted with animal patterns, while others were actually made in the shape of animals such as fish or birds, or humans. The Moche made jewelry from gold, silver, and stones such as turquoise. Examples include ornaments to be worn in a pierced nose, and large ear spools that would have gradually stretched the wearer's earlobes.

THE NAZCA

The Nazca lived in the same area as the Paracas culture, and the two overlapped in time as well. The Nazca first appeared around 200 BCE and lasted until about 600 CE. During this time, their culture was spread out among small villages, each with its own chief. The Nazca traded with other cultures in the Andes for wool, and feathers from rainforest birds have also been found at their sites. Like several of the cultures in the region, the Nazca mummified their dead before placing them in tombs. The dry climate of the Nazca homeland made the process easier.

Nazca culture
c. 500 CE

Andes Mountains

The Nazca made pottery that was often painted in bright colors.

ℂNAZCA LINES

The Nazca are most famous for the huge designs, called geoglyphs, they left behind in the deserts. To make them, they scraped off the surface layer to reveal the lighter rocks beneath. The lines they created were often in the shape of living things, including a hummingbird, a monkey, and a cactus. The carvings are absolutely enormous—the longest straight line is about 12 miles (20 km) and in total, there are over 800 miles (1,300 km) of lines. Historians still aren't sure what they were for. One theory is that people would walk along them as part of a religious ceremony or that they were images for the gods in the sky.

Most of the Nazca line shapes are only visible from the air, but some were carved on hillsides and could be seen from the ground.

THE INCA EMPIRE

Most early South American cultures were loosely organized and didn't rule over particularly large areas. That all changed with the rise of the Inca in the 1400s CE. They built an empire that stretched for thousands of miles along the Pacific coast.

Sacsayhuaman is an Inca temple and fortress complex that overlooks the city of Cuzco.

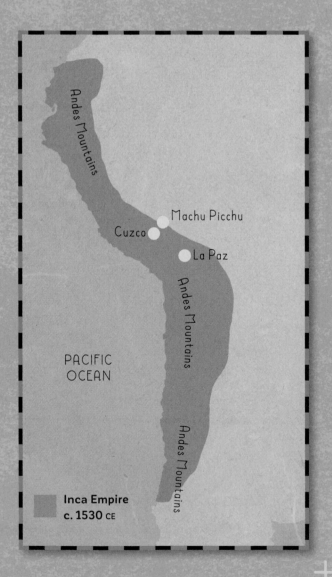

Andes Mountains

Machu Picchu
Cuzco
La Paz

Andes Mountains

PACIFIC OCEAN

Andes Mountains

Inca Empire
c. 1530 CE

RUNNING AN EMPIRE

Pachacuti (above right) set up a system that allowed him to run a large empire from his capital, Cuzco. Conquered peoples had to pay tax in the form of goods or labor. The government used this to build roads and storehouses to protect the food supply. There were thousands of government administrators who each played a part in making sure things ran smoothly.

Remains of an Inca road outside La Paz, Bolivia

HUMBLE BEGINNINGS

According to Inca legend, their people migrated to the valley surrounding the city of Cuzco, in modern-day Peru, sometime before 1200 CE. They pushed out the people living there, then gradually started to expand into the surrounding area. They forced their neighbors to pay them tribute in return for their safety. Over the following years, the Inca territory slowly expanded.

PACHACUTI

Pachacuti Inca Yupanqui was the ninth Inca leader, ruling from 1438–1471 CE. He came to power after successfully defending Cuzco against an attack by the Chanca tribe—legend says that he called on the gods for help, and they turned stones into warriors to help in the fight. Once in power, Pachacuti turned his kingdom into a true empire by conquering lands far beyond the Cuzco valley.

BORN:	DIED:
Before 1438 CE	1471 CE

CUZCO AND MACHU PICCHU

The two most famous Inca sites are very different. Their capital was Cuzco, which at its peak had a population of 150,000. The city is in a valley, surrounded by mountain peaks. It had palaces and temples and was laid out in the form of a puma. The site of Machu Picchu, founded by Pachacuti in around 1450 CE, was much smaller—home to just 1,000 people. This mountaintop site may have been a fortress or a retreat for the emperor, or it may have been mainly a religious site. Both places made use of the Inca technique of cutting stone blocks so precisely that they fitted together without mortar.

After the fall of the Inca, Machu Picchu was abandoned and forgotten, and only rediscovered hundreds of years later.

KEEPING IN TOUCH

Unlike some other early American cultures, the Inca did not have a written language. They used messengers called chasquis to carry messages to all corners of the empire. These runners traveled on foot along the road network, passing their message orally from one runner to the next. The Inca kept records using devices known as quipus, which were made from knotted strings. The colors and knot patterns of each quipu could be used to keep track of dates and accounts, and even to record stories and poetry.

A colorful knotted quipu made by the Inca to keep accounts

INCA RELIGION

The Inca believed in a creator god named Viracocha, who made the first humans as well as the Sun, Moon, and stars. But probably their most important god was Inti, god of the Sun. They saw their emperor as a living descendant of Inti. Every year at the winter solstice, they held a ceremony in his honor known as the Inti Raymi. As part of the ceremony, they offered sacrifices to the earth goddess Pachamama, hoping for a good growing season. Throughout the year, the Inca left offerings at small shrines called huacas, where they believed that gods and spirits were present in the form of natural features.

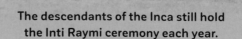
The descendants of the Inca still hold the Inti Raymi ceremony each year.

Inca Art

The Inca were known for their beautiful textiles, made from llama and alpaca wool, and sometimes decorated with feathers. They used weaving and embroidery to make geometric patterns instead of pictures. The Inca were also skilled metalworkers. They believed that gold was the sweat of the Sun, and silver was the tears of the moon. They used these metals to make jewelry, statues, and ceremonial knives for the emperor and his nobles.

Part of the handle of a ceremonial knife made by the Inca

Atahualpa, the last Inca emperor

Enter the Conquistadors

By 1532, the Inca emperor ruled over a huge territory with a population of about 10 million people. But in November of that year, a Spanish treasure-seeker named Francisco Pizarro arrived in the northern Inca city of Cajamarca and met the Inca emperor, Atahualpa. Thanks to their armor, cannons, and horses, Pizarro's small force was able to massacre the Inca soldiers and capture the emperor. Pizarro offered to exchange Atahualpa for a huge amount of gold, which the Inca provided. But Pizarro killed Atahualpa anyway, and his men plundered the empire.

Micronesian house (see page 149)

Wooden malagan carving (see page 148)

MICRONESIA
p149

MELANESIA
p148

NEW ZEALAND
pp154–155

Aboriginal rock art (see page 147)

AUSTRALIA
pp144–147

This map identifies areas within the civilizations and cultures featured in this chapter. Turn to the listed pages to see their full extent and to find out more about them.

MANY ISLANDS

The Pacific Ocean covers about 30 percent of Earth's surface and is dotted with many thousands of islands. Spreading out northwest from the continent of Australia, this island region covers millions of square miles of ocean. People have been using handcrafted boats to travel between these islands for many years, developing a range of fascinating cultures.

HAWAII
p153

THE POLYNESIANS
pp150–155

Moai stone figures on the island of Rapa Nui (see page 152)

RAPA NUI
p152

AUSTRALIA AND OCEANIA

The other five inhabited continents are all connected by land—or at least they were in fairly recent times—so humans could migrate from one to another on foot. But Australia and the islands of Oceania are another story. They could only be settled once humans had mastered the art of traveling by boat.

ANCIENT AUSTRALIA

The land that is now Australia broke off from a giant supercontinent about 30 million years ago. Since then, it has been isolated. Species of plants and animals, such as kangaroos and other marsupials, have evolved here that exist nowhere else on earth. The isolation also means that Australia's human cultures are unique.

COMING TO AUSTRALIA

The first humans to live in Australia probably arrived at least 50,000 years ago. They came from the islands of southeast Asia. Although sea levels were lower back then, and there were more land bridges between islands, many of these journeys would likely have been by boat. The new arrivals gradually spread throughout the continent, and by about 35,000 years ago the whole continent was occupied—including Tasmania, which was part of the mainland until sea levels rose around 10,000 years ago and cut it off.

The first humans in Australia found the continent had many unique animals, including kangaroos (left), koalas (right), and platypuses (below).

Hunting, Gathering, and Farming

The Aboriginal peoples who lived on the Australian mainland had a largely hunter-gatherer lifestyle, using spears and curved throwing sticks called boomerangs to bring down prey. The Aboriginal peoples also managed fire carefully. By deliberately burning an area of scrub, fresh grass would grow and attract grazing kangaroos that they could hunt. There is evidence that they likely also farmed crops such as millet, yams, and nuts.

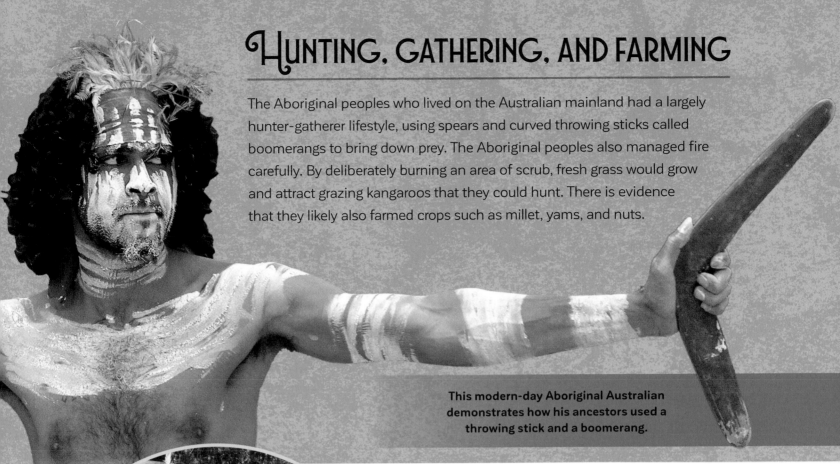

This modern-day Aboriginal Australian demonstrates how his ancestors used a throwing stick and a boomerang.

Modern Torres Strait Islanders perform a traditional dance

Two Groups

The indigenous peoples of Australia are divided into two main groups: the Aboriginal peoples and the Torres Strait Islander peoples. Both groups are deeply connected to the natural world, but each has its own language family and cultural identity. The Torres Strait Islander peoples live on the islands found between Australia's north coast and Papua New Guinea. Before European colonization, they traded a variety of goods with other island communities— anything from feathers and tools to turtle shells and pearls.

European Contact

Those Australian indigenous peoples who lived along the north coast did have contact with other cultures, such as traders from Indonesia. However, groups to the south had no contact with the outside world until British settlers arrived in 1788. Wanting the land and its resources for themselves, the British killed many Aboriginal people and pushed others into the heart of the continent. Thousands more died of diseases brought by the settlers, to which the indigenous peoples had no immunity.

Despite the land already being occupied, Captain James Cook was quick to claim it for Britain when he explored the east coast in 1770.

FAMILY GROUPS

Australia's Aboriginal peoples lived in family groups, which were part of larger groupings that lived in a particular territory and spoke the same language. For most of the year, small groups would travel together, so as not to use up the area's food resources too quickly. But a few times a year, there would be large gatherings with religious activities. In Aboriginal society, extended families often lived close together. People would use the term "father" to refer to their biological father as well as his brothers, and "mother" to refer to their biological mother and her sisters.

This painting shows an Aboriginal encampment in the hills outside Adelaide in the first half of the 19th century.

THE DREAMING

The worldview of the Aboriginal peoples is based on a concept known as the "Dreaming." This is the idea that past, present, and future are all connected to every other aspect of life. It includes the beginning of the world and the mythical beings that created it, as well as the rules that people must follow to keep things going as they are. It is a beginning that never ended. The Aboriginal peoples believe that living people can learn and gain strength from the spirit world through dreams and trances.

SACRED SITES

The Aboriginal peoples passed on stories and knowledge about the Dreaming by word of mouth, from one generation to the next. They also had certain places in the landscape that were seen as sacred. These could include hills, rocks, trees, springs, and plains—any kind of natural feature that had a special connection to the Dreaming and their ancestral beings and stories. For example, the mountain range called the Flinders Ranges is said to be formed by the bodies of two serpents from the Dreaming who ate so many people that they could no longer move.

Aboriginal rock art of a human figure in the Kakadu National Park in the Northern Territory of Australia.

MUSIC AND ART

Much of the art and music produced by Australia's Aboriginal peoples is linked to the Dreaming. Singing and chanting were often accompanied by clapping sticks or wind instruments called didjeridus, made from long hollow branches. Storytellers passed on tales about ancestors as well as everyday life. People used natural pigments such as ocher to paint on rocks, bark, or even on their bodies. Rock paintings often show animals, humans, or handprints.

The rock formation known as Wilpena Pound in the Flinders Ranges is also known by the name Ikara in the Aboriginal Adnyamathanha language, which means "meeting place."

PACIFIC ISLANDS

The Pacific islands east of Indonesia and the Philippines are divided into three main groups. The first is Melanesia, to the northwest of Australia. Micronesia is north of that, and Polynesia—the largest region—lies to the east, extending all the way to Hawaii in the north, Easter Island in the east, and New Zealand to the south (see pages 150–151).

Mariana Islands
MICRONESIA
Palau
Pohnpei
Marshall Islands
Caroline Islands
Kiribati
New Guinea
Solomon Islands
MELANESIA
Vanuatu
Australia
New Caledonia
Fiji
POLYNESIA
New Zealand

MELANESIA

Melanesia was the first of these regions to be settled by humans. There have been people living in the Torres Strait Islands and New Guinea for at least 40,000 years, while the farther islands such as Fiji were settled sometime between 1500 and 1000 BCE. The region's name comes from the Greek for "black islands," a name given by European explorers because of the dark skin of the people who lived there. They lived in small communities based on family groups, and they farmed, hunted, fished, and traded with nearby islands.

Wooden malagan carvings are made by the peoples of the New Ireland region of Papua New Guinea. They're used as part of Malagan ceremonies reinforcing social relationships and responsibilities.

The design of an outrigger canoe is so efficient that people still use them today.

OUTRIGGER CANOES

The earliest boats used by humans were probably made from hollowed tree trunks. But the invention of an improved boat known as an outrigger canoe is the main reason that the Pacific Islands were able to be settled. The main body of the canoe is supported by one or more floats (the outriggers) at the side. The supports make the canoe much more stable in the water, especially when the canoe has a sail. These sorts of boats have been in use since about 3000 BCE.

MICRONESIA

Many of the islands of Micronesia are low coral outcrops that were first settled sometime between 1500 and 1 BCE. The most westerly of the islands were likely to have been first inhabited by people from Taiwan who came via the Philippines. There was a wide range of cultures and languages in this region, but communities were mainly organized into groups led by a chief. There was relatively little land available for farming, so tribes protected and defended what they had.

Micronesian houses are still built in the traditional style using a frame of mahogany and bamboo tied with coconut fibers.

NAN MADOL

On the island of Pohnpei in Micronesia is a city called Nan Madol, built on around 100 artificial islands in a shallow lagoon along the shore. The islands are separated by canals and on them are buildings made of stone. The oldest buildings may date back to around 700 CE, while the more recent ones were built in the 1500s. The city was the capital of a ruling family known as the Saudeleurs.

The Saudeleurs were overthrown by an invasion from a neighboring tribe and Nan Madol was abandoned in the middle of the 1600s.

THE POLYNESIANS

The islands of Polynesia

are spread out over a huge area. Many are small and separated by huge distances. With only canoes to travel in, settling them was a slow process. The islands that now make up New Zealand were the last to be inhabited in around 1250 CE.

MICRONESIA

Hawaii

Christmas Island

Tuvalu

Samoa   POLYNESIA

French Polynesia

MELANESIA

Tonga   Cook Islands

Rapa Nui
Pitcan

New Zealand

THE LAPITA

The first people to settle Polynesia were the Lapita, who originally came from Taiwan and East Asia. They also settled in Melanesia and parts of Micronesia, and they reached western Polynesia sometime before 1000 BCE. Most of what we know about the Lapita comes from the pottery they left behind, which has geometric patterns pressed into the clay. The Lapita also left behind fishhooks and beads and rings made from shells.

POLYNESIAN CULTURE

Polynesian society was divided into social classes, with the chief at the top. Chiefs would lead their people in battle, oversee the sharing out of food and other resources, and communicate with the gods. The Polynesians believed in a supernatural force or energy called mana that flows through living things as well as objects. Mana can be good or evil, and it can be passed on or lost.

Polynesian canoes were powered by sails and paddles.

An example of Lapita pottery

TRAVELING BY CANOE

The Polynesians traveled between islands by canoe. They sometimes used simple outrigger canoes (see page 148), but long journeys often required a double-hulled canoe. These craft were made from two large canoes bound together. A platform spanning the space between them could carry food and other goods. A large double-hulled canoe could carry up to 100 people, along with supplies, such as seeds and farm animals, that they would need when settling a new island.

(see page 148)

Pacific Islanders made maps using sticks, with shells representing the islands, to help them navigate.

NAVIGATION

Unlike most early sailors, the Polynesians didn't hug the coast for safety. Instead, they sailed into the unknown, looking for land that was too far away to see. Polynesian navigators used the position of the stars, the Sun, and the Moon to find their way. They also understood ocean waves and currents, and they used the shapes of clouds and the movement of birds as clues for finding land. Navigators didn't write down their knowledge, but they used stories to pass it down to the next generation.

Rapa Nui

The island of Rapa Nui, also known as Easter Island, is incredibly remote—nearly 1,250 miles (2,000 km) from the nearest Polynesian island and more than 2,175 miles (3,500 km) from the coast of South America. Humans first reached the densely forested island sometime between 800 and 1200 CE, after a journey that would have taken several weeks. The population quickly grew, reaching a height of perhaps 9,000 people by 1550. However, by that time, the people had cut down so many trees that the soil eroded and their crops failed. When European explorers arrived in 1722, there were only about 2,000 people left.

Stone Heads

Rapa Nui is most famous for the hundreds of stone figures, called moai (shown below), that were erected there. Each statue has a very large head and represents an ancestor chief believed to have supernatural powers. The tallest moai was almost 33 ft (10 m) high. They are set on stone platforms called ahu, and most of them are positioned looking inland, as though watching over the people in the villages. It must have taken a huge amount of work to quarry the stone, carve it, then drag it and stand it upright.

In Hawaiian religion, Pele is the goddess of fire and volcanoes, who created the Hawaiian islands.

HAWAII

The Hawaiian Islands are equally remote, lying north of the rest of Polynesia and thousands of miles from mainland Asia and North America. They are the peaks of a chain of undersea mountains, and there are still active volcanoes there. The islands were first settled sometime around 400 CE by people from the Marquesas Islands, then a second group arrived from Tahiti sometime before 1000 CE. These settlers brought their Polynesian culture with them, but Hawaii is so isolated that it soon grew and developed into something unique.

LAND OF RICHES

The Hawaiian Islands are rich in natural resources—rich enough to support a complex society with a large population. The early settlers farmed taro, bananas, coconut, and breadfruit, and they raised pigs and chickens. They built ponds to farm fish, and they collected oysters. Many people lived in towns that would each have had workshops and boathouses, as well as a temple and a house for the chief. A single ruler had power over the whole island, with less important chiefs in charge of villages or districts.

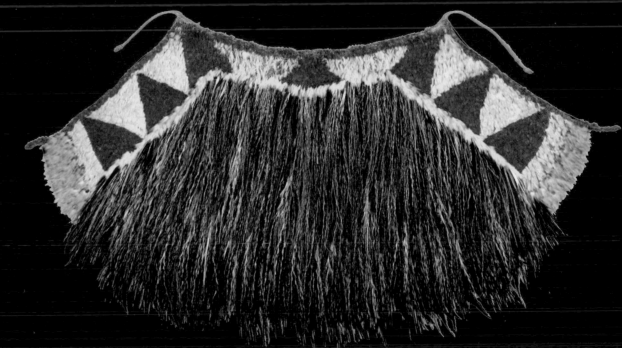

Only high-ranking chiefs wore feathered capes like this one dating from before 1778 CE.

Ancient New Zealand

Of all the places on Earth where people have settled permanently, the islands of New Zealand were probably the last to be occupied. These settlers, the Māori believe, arrived here in around 1250 CE. They found a land of incredible natural beauty, where they set up a thriving culture.

A modern Māori performing a haka

The Legend of Kupe

The Māori believe they came from a land called Hawaiki. Its location has never been pinpointed, and it may be a mythical place. Māori legends tell of a man named Kupe, who set off from Hawaiki in a canoe. After adventures, such as chasing a giant octopus, he landed on the shores of Aotearoa—the Māori name for New Zealand, meaning "land of the long white cloud." Telling the story of Kupe was a way for the first peoples of New Zealand to pass on the knowledge of stars, winds, and navigation.

Examples of Māori rock art near Duntroon, New Zealand dating from 1400–1900 CE

The Māori

The earliest settlers are known as the Māori. They may have originally come from the Polynesian island of Tahiti, though no one knows for sure. The Māori hunted and grew crops such as yams. They were divided into groups called hapu, each led by a chief. In times of war, several hapus would join together to form a larger tribe called an iwi. They built fortified settlements on hilltops for protection. Battles were fought according to strict rules and a dance, known as the haka, was performed before a battle to show a tribe's strength. Hakas are still performed by some New Zealand sports teams today.

Moa were bigger than ostriches, and the Māori hunted them with spears or by setting traps.

Natural Wonders

Most Polynesian islands are small, but Aotearoa is huge, with a varied landscape that includes mountains and glaciers as well as forests and long stretches of coastline. It was home to animals such as the moa, an enormous flightless bird that was hunted to extinction by around 1500 CE. The Māori also hunted sea animals such as whales and seals. Their lifestyle and religion were closely linked to the natural environment around them.

Māori Art

New Zealand is colder than most other parts of Polynesia. To keep warm, the Māori wove fibers from the flax plant into cloaks and other items. Each pattern in the cloth has its own meaning. The Māori also carve traditional images and patterns into wood, bone, and a type of green stone called pounamu. These carvings often have a spiritual significance. Māori are also well known for intricate tattoos on their faces and bodies. The tattoos are a rite of passage and show a person's connection to their family and heritage.

An intricate Māori wood carving from the early 18th century.

TIMELINE

Western Asia

Central, Southern, and Eastern Asia

Europe

Africa

North America

South America

Australia and Oceania

c. 3300 BCE: Sumerian civilization emerges

c. 3600 BCE: the first silk is made in China

c. 3200 BCE: Newgrange tomb is built in Ireland and standing stones are erected at Carnac in France

1050–221 BCE: Zhou Dynasty rules China

c. 3800 BCE: the city of Ur is founded

c. 1380 BCE: The Hittite Empire is at its height

c. 14,000–300 BCE: Jōmon culture grows in Japan

c. 3000–1520 BCE: Stonehenge is built

c. 1600 –1046 BCE: The Shang Dynasty rules in China

c. 5400 BCE: Eridu is founded

c. 1700 BCE: Nordic people are making bronze weapons and tools

c. 6000 BCE: first settlements are founded in Korea

c. 2000 BCE: The old Assyrian Empire flourishes

c. 2000 BCE: The Minoan palace civilization emerges in Crete

c. 7000 BCE: people begin farming along the Indus River

c. 2300 BCE: The Akkadian Empire thrives

c. 12,000 years ago: farming begins in the fertile crescent in Mesopotamia

c. 2500 BCE: Mohenjo-daro is founded in the Indus Valley

c. 5000 BCE: Nubian farming communities are established on the River Nile

c. 2600 BCE: pharaohs begin to build stone pyramids in Egypt

c. 1700 BCE: the epic of Gilgamesh is created

c. 2800 BCE: Eridu is flooded

c. 40,000 years ago: people settled in the Torres Strait Islands and New Guinea

1539 BCE: New Kingdom period begins in Egypt

65,000–50,000 years ago: people first come to Australia

c. 1500–1000 BCE: Islands in Melanesia are settled

c. 3500–1500 BCE: groups in Peru including the Caral-Supe are building settlements

c. 1500–400 BCE: The Olmecs flourish in Mexico

◄——— 15,000 BCE–4000 BCE ———►   4000 BCE–1 BCE ———

c. 800 BCE: The new Assyrian Empire is growing

49 BCE: Julius Caesar takes control of Rome

c. 25–220 CE: The first paper is made in China

c. 900 CE: The Toltec Empire rises

1519: Spanish invaders begin the conquest of the Aztec Empire

c. 130 BCE: The Silk Road grows as a trade route

98–117 CE: The Roman Empire reaches its greatest extent during the reign of Trajan

336–323 BCE: Alexander the Great conquers stretches of Europe, Asia, and Africa

c. 750 CE: Ancestral Puebloan culture thrives in southwestern USA

322–185 BCE: The Mauryan Empire rules in India

c. 700 CE: Mound building peoples are living in eastern USA

c. 320 BCE–550 BCE: The Gupta Empire grows in India

c. 600–1200 CE: the Maya city of Chichén Itzá is thriving in Mexico

c. 1500: Europeans arrive in North America, coming into contact with Native American peoples

700s BCE: Athens, Sparta, Corinth, and Thebes are powerful Greek city-states

c. 500 CE: The Celtic culture is spreading across Europe

c. 400 CE: The Vandals and Visigoth tribes are pushing into Europe

c. 1100 CE: Angkor Wat temple is built

753 BCE: Rome is founded, according to legend

c. 200 CE: The Teotihuacan people are living in central Mexico

c. 1300 CE: The Aztec Empire controls large parts of Mesoamerica

c. 553 BCE: beginning of the first Persian Empire

c. 1100 CE: the city of Great Zimbabwe is built

712 BCE: Kushites conquer Egypt

c. 500 CE: The Moche culture flourishes in northern Peru

c. 1250 CE: New Zealand is settled

c. 400 CE: the islands of Hawaii are settled

c. 1300 CE: stone heads are carved by the Rapa Nui people

1400s: The Inca Empire rules large parts of South America

814 BCE: the city of Carthage is founded, according to legend

c. 250 CE: the "golden age" of the Maya begins

146 BCE: Rome defeats Carthage

c. 750 CE: Lapita people come to Polynesia from East Asia

1450 CE: Machu Picchu is founded

c. 900–400 BCE: The Chavín and Paracas people are living on the Pacific coast, west of the Andes Mountains

c. 200 BCE–600 CE: The Nazca are making pottery and geoglyphs

c. 100 CE: The Kingdom of Axum rises

c. 800 CE: The Ghana Empire flourishes

1532: Spanish invaders begin the conquest of the Inca Empire

1 CE–1532 CE

GLOSSARY

aqueduct A structure built to carry water from its source to where it is needed

archaeologist A person who uncovers and studies objects and other remains left behind by people who lived in the past

artifact An object created by humans, often one of cultural interest or importance

BCE An abbreviation of "Before the Common Era"—a way of defining a time period based on the traditionally recognized year of the birth of Jesus

Bronze Age A time in the past when bronze was the most common material used for making tools and weapons; the Bronze Age happened at different times in different places

Buddhism A religion founded in the late 6th century BCE based on the teachings of the Buddha, whose followers believe that spiritual improvement will lead to an escape from human suffering

burial mound A mound of earth built over one or more graves; many different cultures have used burial mounds

c. An abbreviation of the term "circa," which means "approximately"; it is usually used before a date to suggest that it is an estimate

CE An abbreviation of "Common Era"—a period of time after the commonly recognized birth of Jesus

civilization A group of people that farms the land, builds and inhabits cities, has a social hierarchy, and is ruled by some form of government

cuneiform A type of writing used long ago in Western Asia, based on wedge-shaped symbols pressed into damp clay

Dark Age A term used to describe a time in the past when culture and society declined, or a time when the history is unknown because of a lack of written records

the Dreaming The worldview of the Aboriginal peoples of Australia, which recalls a time when the land was inhabited by ancestral figures

empire A collection of countries or kingdoms ruled by a single person or government

excavate To dig into the ground looking for clues about life in the past

glyph A picture or symbol that represents a word, used in some ancient writing systems

hieroglyphs Pictorial characters used for writing by the Egyptians (and other cultures)

hoard A collection of valuable artifacts, such as coins or jewelry, found buried together

Homo sapiens The species name used to describe modern humans

hunter-gatherers People who live by hunting and collecting wild food, rather than by raising crops and livestock

ice age A time in the past when Earth was colder and large masses of ice covered much of the land

Iron Age A time in the past when iron was the most common material used for making tools and weapons; the Iron Age happened at different times in different places

jade A naturally-occurring green stone, often used to make jewelry or special objects

labyrinth A confusing set of connecting passages, like a maze

longhouse A long, narrow house that provided living space for several families or even a whole community; many different cultures around the world have built longhouses

mica A crystal-like mineral used by ancient civilizations to make pottery

midden A heap where people in the past tossed waste such as bones, shells, and broken pottery

Middle East The area where Europe, Africa, and Asia meet

mosaic A pattern or picture made using many small pieces of colored stone or glass

mummy The body of a human or animal that has been preserved by chemicals, lack of air, or extreme dryness or cold

nomadic Moving from one place to another (often following food sources) instead of living in one place all the time

obelisk A tall stone column with a pointed top, made in honor of an important person or event

obsidian A type of glassy rock formed from cooling lava, which forms sharp edges when it breaks and can be made into tools and weapons

pharaoh The title given to kings in ancient Egypt; both male and female rulers used this title

philosopher A person who studies or writes about the meaning of life

pyramid A large structure with a triangular shape, often built as a temple or tomb

sarcophagus A stone coffin, often richly carved or decorated

script A writing system consisting of an alphabet or a set of symbols that represent sounds or words

seal An object used to make an official mark on a document

smelting The process by which metals are melted to separate their elements or rocks are heated to extract the metal they contain

standing stone A large stone placed upright in the ground; standing stones often appear in groups to mark sites that were important to ancient people

ziggurat A large terraced temple structure built by the ancient Mesopotamians

INDEX

ACKNOWLEDGMENTS

The publishers would like to thank the following sources for their kind permission to reproduce the pictures in this book. The page numbers for each of the photographs are listed below, giving the page on which they appear in the book and any location indicator (c-center, t-top, b-bottom, l-left, r-right).

CREDITS

Alamy: 47tr Suzuki Kaku/Alamy Stock Photo, 124tl PRISMA ARCHIVO/Alamy Stock Photo, 126bl Mark Burnett / Alamy Stock Photo, 132c Album / Alamy Stock Photo, 135t Album / Alamy Stock Photo, 141br Dick S. Ramsay Fund, Mary Smith Dorward Fund, Marie Bernice Bitzer Fund, Frank L. Babbott Fund; Gift of The Roebling Society and the American Art Council; purchased with funds given by an anonymous donor, Maureen and Marshall Cogan, Karen B. Cohen, Georgia and Michael deHavenon, Harry Kahn, Alastair B. Martin, Ted and Connie Roosevelt, Frieda and Milton F. Rosenthal, Sol Schreiber in memory of Ann Schreiber, Joanne Witty and Eugene Keilin, Thomas L. Pulling, Roy J. Zuckerberg, Kitty and Herbert Glantz, Ellen and Leonard L. Milberg, Paul and Thérèse Bernbach, Emma and J. A. Lewis, Florence R. Kingdon.

Creative Commons: 10tr Nandaro/Creative Commons, 17bl Mikelzubi/Creative Commons, 19tr Hans Ollermann/Creative Commons, 20bl Zunkir/Creative Commons, 21c Mark Ahsmann/Creative Commons, 21r Unknown Author/Creative Commonsl, 22br Osama Shukir Muhammed Amin FRCP(Glasg)/Creative Commons, 24tr Osama Shukir Muhammed Amin FRCP(Glasg)/Creative Commons, 25tr Fletcher Fund, 1947/Creative Commons, 26bl Hans Ollerman/Creative Commons, 27tr Mefman00/Creative Commons, 27br Osama Shukir Muhammed Amin FRCP(Glasg)/Creative Commons, 29tr Mbzt/Creative Commons, 29c The U.S. Army/Creative Commons, 30-31b Rictor Norton/Creative Commons, 37c Marco Prins/Creative Commons, 37r CNG coins/Creative Commons, 38tl Prioryman/Creative Commons, 38b National Museums Scotland/Creative Commons, 40b Surenae/Creative Commons, 40r Nasser-sadeghi/Creative Commons, 42l Gary Todd/Creative Commons, 43r Rogers Fund, 1918/Commons Creative, 45b Gary Todd/Creative Commons, 51b Creative Commons, 55b British Library/Creative Commons/Public Domain, 56tr Dr. Schul/Creative Commons, 57bl Rogers Fund, 1918/Creative Commons, 64t Nationalmuseet/Creative Commons, 67tr Creative Commons, 69tl © Marie-Lan Nguyen/Wikimedia Commons/CC-BY 2.5, 74bl Caeciliusinhorto/Creative Commons, 74br George E. Koronaios/Creative Commons, 75tl Ancient Agora Museum, Athens/Creative Commons ,75t http://ohiostatehouse.org, 79br Creative Commons, 81b Sailko/Creative Commons, 81tr Creative Commons, 82-83 Regien Paassen, 83l Vladimir Korostyshevskiy, 83c Yaroslaff, 83 I. Pilon, 84cl Bertl123, 84bl J J Osuna Caballero, 84br 3drenderings, 85t Staatliche Graphische Sammlung München, Inventar-Nr. 95013, 86-7 PHGCOM/Creative Commons, 87b Aerial video capture/Creative Commons, 89tr Á. M. Felicísimo /Creative Commons, 89c Walters Art Museum/Creative Commons, 90 Joe Mabel/Creative Commons, 91t National Museum of Denmark, 92bl, 101r Franko Khoury/public domain, 92c Tangopaso/Smithsonian National Museum of African Art, 96c The Yorck Project (2002) , 101b Hans Ollerman/Creative Commons, 102l Ermitage/Public domain, 103r Yale University Art Gallery/Public domain, 103c Jastrow/ From the Gardens of the Tuileries, 1872, 104-105t Classical Numismatic Group, inc.http://www.cngcoins.com, 104b Elitre/Creative Commons, 109tr Gallica Digital Library, 112tr dalbera/Creative Commons, 114tl Hiart/Creative Commons, 125tr Codex Mendoza/Public Domain, 125cr Purchase, 2015 Benefit Fund and Lila Acheson Wallace Gift, 2016, 131tl Nationalmuseet - National Museum of Denmark/Creative Commons, 131tr Creative Commons, 131br USCapitol/Public Domain, 132l Patrick Charpiat/Creative Commons, 136b Patrick Charpiat/Creative Commons, 142c Fanny Schertzer/Creative Commons, 146t Art Gallery of South Australia/Public Domain, 148bl Fanny Schertzer/Creative Commons, 150bl Torbenbrinker/Creative Commons, 150-151b Makthorpe/Public Domain, 151tr Cullen328/Creative Commons, 153b Australian Museum/Creative Commons, 154t Steve Evans/Creative Commons, 155br Museopedia/Creative Commons

Shutterstock: 6-7 Guenter Albers, 7l Mark Green, 7r Kanuman, 10 bl Anton_Ivanov, 11tr Nitr, 12 Ivan Soto Cobos, 13t soozi imer, 13b Fedor Selivanov, 14l Shan_shan, 14r Shan_shan, 15tr Denys Dolnikov, 15bl Kamira, 16bl Mlle Sonyah, 17tr MNStudio, 18tr Alvaro Lovazzano, 19br Simon Edge, 23tl Dima Moroz, 23br Simon Edge, 24bl Will Rodrigues, 25br Vladimir Korostyshevskiy, 28-29b 3DF mediaStudio, 30t Dima Moroz, 31c AstralManSigmaDelta, 31t German Vizulis, 32t Nicku, 32b silverfox999, 33b GIGASHOTS, 34bl Pogorelova Olga, 35b MysticaLink, 36l Alvaro Lovazzano, 36-37b hemro, 37tr wjarek, 39t Oddai, 38-39b TripDeeDee Photo, 41t Sulo Letta, 41b Massimo Pizzotti, 42r Oleskaus, 43tr Nanocent, 43b Shan_shan, 44l Iftekkhar, 45t AlexelA, 46t DARSHAN KUMAR, 46b SantanuU, 47b DARSHAN KUMAR, 48 saiko3p, 49 Hari Mahidhar, 50 Danny Ye, 51l Suchat tepruang, 51r aphotostory, 52bl lady-luck, 52-53b Kanuman, 53tl aphotostory, 53br Mark Brandon, 54tl Andrea Paggiaro, 54cr Svet_Zhdan, 54bl Shan_shan, 55tl cl2004lhy, 56l Keitma, 56bc Nanocent, 57tr Satoshi.RR, 57t saiglobalnt, 57br Nisseikikaku, 58-59b Oleskaus, 59r Chakroval, 60-61 Andreas Wolochow, 61br Cholpan, 62t Boris Rezvantsev, 62-63b V. Smirnov, 63 Maykova Galina, 64b MisterStock, 65cl Andreas Wolochow, 65br Dima Moroz, 66cl travellight, 66b MNStudio, 67br Mr Nai, 68 Pecold, 69 Georgios Tsichlis, 70 Sergii Figurnyi, 71c Dima Moroz, 72 Drozdin Vladimir, 73 Gilmanshin , 74t Josep Curto, 75bl Aerial-motion, 75br Aerial-motion, 76tl Carmen Ruiz, 76-77b Aerial-motion, 77t Viacheslav Lopatin, 77b Dima Moroz, 78bl Francesco Cantone, 78br Andreas Wolochow, 80bl ded pixto, 80tr MisterStock, 85b B.Stefanov, 87t Chris Lawrence Travel, 88 Jean-Michel Girard, 91b Frank Bach, 92tr Jaroslav Moravcik, 93t Sergey-73, 93b agap, 94-95 Benvenuto Cellini, 95tc doleesi, 95r mareandmare, 96b Ihor Bondarenko, 97tl Macrovector, 97tr Zvereva Yana, 97b Antonio Petrone, 98-99t Marti Bug Catcher, 98c Andrea Izzotti, 98b Jaroslav Moravcik, 99c Vladimir Melnik, 99br Gokhan Dogan, 100-101c Martchan, 100b hecke61, 103b Valery Bareta, 105b Sergey-73, 106-107 Grace Wangui, 107b Magdalena Paluchowska, 108-109 DemarK, 110 Davide Bonora , 111c evenfh, 111tr evenfh, 111br agap, 112cr Sopotnicki, 112cl delcarmat, 112bl Dmitry Rukhlenko, 113tr Kent Raney, 113br Mardoz, 114-115b Matt Gush, 115 JC Gonram, 116l Alfredo Matus, 116-117 MikeDP, 117tl Mardoz, 117tr A. Skromnitsky, 118tl Leonard G., 118bl WH_Pics, 118-119 buteo, 119tr Valentyn Volkov, 119cr Diego Grandi, 119br Kiev.Victor, 120bl Dmitry Rukhlenko, 120r clicksdemexico, 121bl Chepe Nicoli, 121br FootageLab, 122tl Magi Bagi, 122-123b darko m, 123tr delcarmat, 123r Peter Hermes Furian, 124bl Mistervlad, 125br Grigory Kubatyan, 127tr TimVickers, 127c Kent Raney, 128bl Sopotnicki, 128-129 Bob Adams, Albuquerque, NM, 130bl SF Photo, 132r videobuzzing, 133 casa.da.photo, 134-135b Christian Vinces, 135r Jess Kraft, 136t Andreas Wolochow, 137t Myriam B, 137b deobuzzing, 138t Myriam B, 138b Jess Kraft, 139t lovelypeace, 139b Pyty, 140t Simon Mayer, 140b Mark Green, 141tl casa.da.photo, 142tc maloff, 142b Miroslaw Skorka, 143r Gabor Kovacs Photography, 144bl Smileus, 144bc Vac1, 144br Eric Isselee, 145tl ChameleonsEye, 145cl ChameleonsEye, 145br fibPhoto, 146-147b B J Casey Photography58, 147tr Miroslaw Skorka, 149t maloff, 149b KKKvintage, 152 Gabor Kovacs Photography, 153t orxy, 154b trabantos

Courtesy of: 141br Dick S. Ramsay Fund, Mary Smith Dorward Fund, Marie Bernice Bitzer Fund, Frank L. Babbott Fund; Gift of The Roebling Society and the American Art Council; purchased with funds given by an anonymous donor, Maureen and Marshall Cogan, Karen B. Cohen, Georgia and Michael deHavenon, Harry Kahn, Alastair B. Martin, Ted and Connie Roosevelt, Frieda and Milton F. Rosenthal, Sol Schreiber in memory of Ann Schreiber, Joanne Witty and Eugene Keilin, Thomas L. Pulling, Roy J. Zuckerberg, Kitty and Herbert Glantz, Ellen and Leonard L. Milberg, Paul and Thérèse Bernbach, Emma and J. A. Lewis, Florence R. Kingdon.

Every effort has been made to acknowledge correctly and contact the source and/or copyright holder of each picture. Any unintentional errors or omissions will be corrected in future editions of this book.